5 DIFFERENT BONUSES IN THIS BOOK

EOE DIET

COOKBOOK

AN ELIMINATION DIET DESIGNED TO MANAGE EOE AND OTHER FOOD ALLERGIES WITH GLUTEN FREE , EGG-FREE , SOY-FREE AND NUT-FREE MEALS (6FED) . FEATURES RECIPES FOCUSED ON GRAINS, LEAFY GREENS , VEGETABLES , MEAT AND POULTRY, CUPCAKES AND MUFFINS .

BY SOPHIA J. CAMPBELL

1 |EOSINOPHILIC ESOPHAGITIS DIET COOKBOOK.

EOE (Eosinophilic Esophagitis) DIET COOKBOOK

An Elimination Diet Designed to Manage EOE and Other Food Allergies with Gluten-Free, Diary-Free, Egg-Free, Fish-Free, Soy-Free, and Nut-Free Meals (6FED). Features Recipes Focused on Grains, Leafy Greens, Vegetables, Meat and Poultry, Cupcakes and Muffins. 5 EXTRA BONUSES.

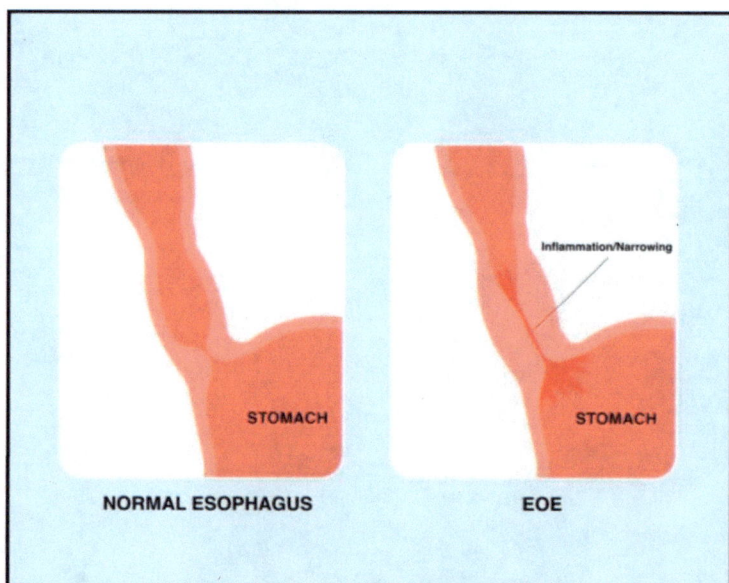

NORMAL ESOPHAGUS

EOE

Inflammation/Narrowing

STOMACH

STOMACH

BY SOPHIA J. CAMPBELL

HOW TO USE THIS COOKBOOK

Here's a simple guide in 5 easy steps on how to use this EOE Diet Cookbook effectively:

1. Understand Your Dietary Restrictions:

- Begin by familiarizing yourself with your specific dietary restrictions related to Eosinophilic Esophagitis (EOE) and other food allergies. Take note of the allergens you need to avoid, such as gluten, dairy, eggs, fish, soy, and nuts, as outlined in the 6FED approach.

2. Browse and Plan:

- Thoroughly explore the EOE Diet Cookbook. Take note of recipes that align with your dietary needs and preferences. Consider planning your meals for the week in advance to ensure a well-balanced and varied diet.

3. Prepare a Shopping List:

- Once you've selected the recipes you want to try, create a shopping list with all the necessary ingredients. Ensure that your pantry is stocked with essential items like gluten-free grains, dairy-free alternatives, egg substitutes, and allergen-free protein sources like poultry or meat.

4. Follow the Recipes Carefully:

- As you begin cooking, follow the cookbook's recipes meticulously. Pay attention to portion sizes, cooking times, and any specific instructions regarding allergen substitutes. The cookbook is designed to provide safe and delicious alternatives, so trust the process and enjoy experimenting with new flavors.

5. Monitor Your Body's Response:

- After incorporating meals from the EOE Diet Cookbook into your routine, pay close attention to your body's response. Note any changes in symptoms or how you feel overall. This step is crucial in determining the effectiveness of the cookbook in managing your EOE and food allergies. Consult with your healthcare provider if needed.

By following these five steps, you can make the most of your EOE Diet Cookbook, making meal planning and preparation a seamless and enjoyable part of managing your dietary requirements.

ACKNOWLEDEMENTS

A Heartfelt thanks to my amazing husband, whose unwavering support fueled this cookbook's creation. Your encouragement and belief in my mission are my driving force. To my little inspiration, my 5-year-old daughter, your joy lights up my world. This cookbook is dedicated to you and all families facing Eosinophilic Esophagitis challenges.

A special shoutout to the resilient EOE community – your strength is truly inspiring. Big thanks to co-workers, friends, and family for understanding and accommodating my dietary needs. Your thoughtfulness during gatherings, picnics, and even Thanksgiving hasn't gone unnoticed. To my supportive friends and family throughout the writing process, your encouragement kept me going.

May this cookbook be a source of inspiration and support for those navigating the complexities of EOE and food allergies.

TABLE OF CONTENTS

INTRODUCTION

In the hushed corners of kitchens worldwide, a quiet revolution is stirring—a revolution born out of the shared challenges faced by those living with Eosinophilic Esophagitis (EOE). Imagine, for a moment, the echo of footsteps in a grocery store, where every label becomes a decipherable code, and the mere thought of dining out feels like navigating a culinary minefield.

Now, let me transport you into the heart of a home, where a family gathers around the table, the air saturated with tantalizing aromas. But for those managing EOE, this idyllic scene often conceals a tapestry of fears and concerns. Will today's meal provoke a reaction? Is it possible to indulge in the joy of food without triggering discomfort?

This cookbook is more than a collection of recipes; it's a lifeline, a testament to the understanding that every meal carries with it a unique set of challenges and dreams. As you hold this book in your hands, know that it was conceived in kitchens echoing with the laughter, frustrations, and triumphs of individuals facing the daily complexities of EOE.

Picture this: A mother, wrestling with the worry of providing nutritious meals for her child, discovers a recipe that not only aligns with dietary restrictions but is embraced with joy by the entire family. Or a young professional, navigating the intricacies of a social event, finds solace in a collection of recipes that promise both safety and indulgence.

We delve into the pages of this cookbook not merely as creators but as companions on your journey toward a life where dietary constraints are not chains but stepping stones to a world of culinary possibilities. As you traverse the chapters ahead, consider each recipe as a beacon, guiding you through a labyrinth of flavors, textures, and nourishment.

This book is your invitation to a culinary revolution—a revolution fueled by the desire for a life rich in flavor, unencumbered by the constraints of EOE. The stories within these pages are not just ours; they're yours, a mirror reflecting the shared hopes, fears, and the unyielding spirit of those embracing a life with Eosinophilic Esophagitis. So, let this introduction be more than just words on a page. Let it be a promise—a promise that within these recipes lies not only the assurance of allergen-free dining but a roadmap to a better, more flavorful life. Step into the revolution. Your journey begins now.

CHAPTER ONE– Understanding EOE

Eosinophilic Esophagitis (EOE) is an immune-mediated disorder causing inflammation in the esophagus. Common symptoms include difficulty swallowing, persistent heartburn, and abdominal pain. Diagnosis involves endoscopy and biopsy, and management may include elimination diets, medications, and nutritional guidance. Living with EOE requires a holistic approach, including psychosocial support. Ongoing research and advocacy aim to enhance awareness and improve the quality of life for those with Eosinophilic Esophagitis.

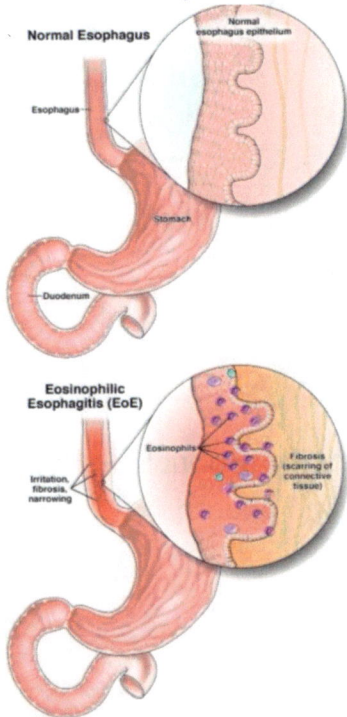

An Overview of the 6FED Approach

The 6FED (Six Food Elimination Diet) approach is a targeted dietary strategy designed to manage Eosinophilic

Esophagitis (EOE) by eliminating six common food allergens. This approach focuses on removing gluten, dairy, eggs, fish, soy, and nuts from the diet, aiming to reduce inflammation and ease symptoms associated with EOE.

Key Components of the 6FED Approach:

1. Gluten-Free: Cutting out gluten-containing grains like wheat, barley, and rye.

2. Dairy-Free: Eliminating dairy products to avoid potential allergens like milk and cheese.

3. Egg-Free: Removing eggs and egg-based products from the diet.

4. Fish-Free: Omitting fish and seafood to prevent allergic reactions.

5. Soy-Free: Avoiding soy products, a common allergen present in many processed foods.

6. Nut-Free: Stepping away from tree nuts and peanuts, which can trigger allergic responses.

Implementation of the 6FED Approach:

1. Identifying Trigger Foods: Work with healthcare professionals to pinpoint specific trigger foods through an elimination diet or allergy testing.

2. Meal Planning: Crafting meals focused on grains, leafy greens, vegetables, meat, and poultry to ensure a balanced and allergen-free diet.

3. Label Reading: Developing a keen eye for reading food labels to identify and avoid hidden allergens.

4. Nutritional Support: Collaborating with a registered dietitian for guidance on maintaining nutritional balance while adhering to the 6FED approach.

Benefits of the 6FED Approach:

1. Symptom Management: Reduction of eosinophilic inflammation in the esophagus, leading to improved symptoms.

2. Personalized Diet: Tailoring the diet to individual sensitivities, providing a customized approach to EOE management.

3. Enhanced Quality of Life: Offering a practical and sustainable way to enjoy a diverse range of foods while managing EOE.

The 6FED approach is a strategic and personalized dietary plan designed to empower individuals with

Eosinophilic Esophagitis. By understanding and implementing the 6FED principles, individuals can take proactive steps towards symptom relief and improved overall well-being.

Identifying your Dietary Restrictions

Identifying Your Dietary Restrictions: Navigating the Path to EOE Management

Identifying your dietary restrictions is a pivotal step in effectively managing Eosinophilic Esophagitis (EOE). This process involves a combination of self-awareness, observation, and professional guidance to pinpoint specific trigger foods and allergens. Here's a concise guide to help you navigate and understand your dietary restrictions:

1. Symptom Tracking:

- Keep a detailed journal of your eating habits and symptoms. Note any discomfort, difficulty swallowing, or other reactions after meals.

2. Professional Guidance:

- Consult with a healthcare professional, preferably a gastroenterologist or allergist, to discuss your symptoms and explore potential food allergens.

3. Allergy Testing:

- Undergo specific allergy tests, such as skin prick tests or blood tests, to identify potential triggers and narrow down the list of allergens affecting you.

4. Elimination Diet:

- Consider implementing an elimination diet under the supervision of a registered dietitian. This involves systematically removing suspected allergens from your diet and reintroducing them one at a time to observe reactions.

5. Endoscopy and Biopsy:

- If necessary, your healthcare provider may recommend an endoscopy with biopsy to visually inspect the esophagus and gather tissue samples for a more accurate diagnosis.

6. Stay Informed:

- Educate yourself on common food allergens, especially those associated with EOE, such as gluten, dairy, eggs, fish, soy, and nuts. Learn to recognize these ingredients on food labels.

7. Listen to Your Body:

- Pay attention to your body's signals. If certain foods consistently lead to discomfort or symptoms, it's crucial to acknowledge and avoid them.

8. Collaborate with Professionals:

- Work closely with a registered dietitian specializing in food allergies and EOE. They can provide personalized guidance, helping you navigate a balanced and allergen-free diet.

By actively identifying your dietary restrictions, you empower yourself to make informed choices that contribute to the effective management of Eosinophilic Esophagitis. Remember that this process is unique to each individual, and the journey toward understanding your dietary needs is a crucial step on the path to improved well-being.

Kitchen Essentials for an EOE Friendly Kitchen

Kitchen Essentials for an EOE-Friendly Kitchen: Crafting a Safe Culinary Haven

Creating an Eosinophilic Esophagitis (EOE)-friendly kitchen involves strategic choices to ensure a safe and allergen-conscious cooking environment. Here's a concise guide to the essential elements that will transform your kitchen into a haven for managing EOE:

1. Dedicated Utensils and Cookware:

- Invest in separate utensils, cutting boards, and cookware to avoid cross-contamination. This includes knives, spatulas, and pots exclusively designated for allergen-free meal preparation.

2. Food Processor or Blender:

- Equip your kitchen with a food processor or blender to create purees and alternatives for certain allergens. These can be essential for crafting flavorful sauces and textures without compromising on safety.

3. Allergen-Free Ingredients Stock:

- Maintain a well-stocked pantry with allergen-free staples, including gluten-free flours, dairy alternatives, egg substitutes, and soy-free sauces. This ensures you have the necessary ingredients for EOE-friendly recipes.

4. Label-Reading Toolkit:

- Develop an eager and anxious eye for reading food labels. Keep a magnifying glass handy to scrutinize ingredient lists for hidden allergens, ensuring your chosen products align with your dietary restrictions.

5. Separate Storage Areas:

- Designate specific areas in your pantry and refrigerator for allergen-free items. This minimizes the risk of accidental exposure and makes it easier to locate the ingredients you need.

6. Meal Prep Containers:

- Invest in a set of airtight meal prep containers to store homemade allergen-free meals and snacks. This not only streamlines your meal planning but also safeguards against cross-contamination in the refrigerator.

7. Educational Resources:

- Keep educational resources, such as cookbooks focused on EOE-friendly recipes, nutrition guides, and allergen substitution charts, within easy reach. These references provide inspiration and guidance for crafting diverse and safe meals.

8. Allergen-Free Cleaning Supplies:

- Ensure your cleaning supplies are allergen-free. Go for hypoallergenic dish soap, surface cleaners, and sponges to maintain a clean and safe kitchen environment.

9. Regular Pantry Audits:

- Conduct regular audits of your pantry to check expiration dates and replace any items that may have expired. This ensures the freshness and safety of your allergen-free ingredients.

10. Communication:

- Establish open communication with family members or housemates about the importance of maintaining an allergen-free kitchen. Encourage collaboration in keeping the space safe for everyone.

By curating your kitchen with these essentials, you lay the foundation for a culinary space that not only caters to the unique needs of Eosinophilic Esophagitis but also fosters a creative and enjoyable cooking experience.

Planning your Meals- A Step by Step Guide

Planning Your Meals: A Step-by-Step Guide for EOE Management

Efficient meal planning is a cornerstone of successfully managing Eosinophilic Esophagitis (EOE), ensuring that each dish is not only safe but also satisfies your nutritional needs. Follow this step-by-step guide to streamline your meal planning process:

1. Identify Your Dietary Restrictions:

- Begin by understanding your specific dietary restrictions. Note allergens to avoid, such as gluten, dairy, eggs, fish, soy, and nuts – key elements in the 6FED approach.

2. Consult a Registered Dietitian:

- Collaborate with a registered dietitian specializing in EOE to create a tailored meal plan. They can provide valuable insights on nutritional balance and guide you in crafting a diverse and allergen-free diet.

3. Create a Weekly Meal Calendar:

- Outline a weekly calendar that includes breakfast, lunch, dinner, and snacks. This provides a visual overview of your meals and ensures variety throughout the week.

4. Focus on Nutrient-Rich Ingredients:

- Emphasize nutrient-dense options such as fruits, vegetables, lean proteins, and gluten-free grains. These form the foundation of a balanced and healthful EOE-friendly diet.

5. Diversify Protein Sources:

- Incorporate a variety of proteins like poultry, lean meats, tofu, and legumes. This not only adds flavor to your meals but also ensures a range of essential nutrients.

6. Explore Alternative Grains:

- Experiment with gluten-free grains like quinoa, rice, millet, and buckwheat. These grains contribute to the diversity of your diet while adhering to EOE restrictions.

7. Prep Allergen-Free Snacks:

- Prepare allergen-free snacks in advance to have on hand when hunger strikes. This prevents reliance on potentially problematic convenience foods.

8. Batch Cooking for Efficiency:

- Consider batch cooking certain components of meals, such as grains, proteins, or sauces. This simplifies daily meal preparation and saves time in the kitchen.

9. Label-Check Ingredients:

- Before shopping, meticulously check labels for allergens. Ensure that the products you choose align with your dietary restrictions to avoid any accidental exposures.

10. Stay Seasonally Inspired:

- Infuse variety into your meals by incorporating seasonal fruits and vegetables. Seasonal produce not only adds freshness but also introduces diverse flavors to your palate.

11. Rotate Recipes Weekly:

- Rotate recipes to prevent culinary monotony. This keeps meals exciting and ensures a well-rounded intake of nutrients.

12. Reflect and Adjust:

- Regularly reflect on your meals and their impact on your health. Adjust your meal plan as needed, considering any new insights or recommendations from your healthcare team.

By following this step-by-step guide, you can create a thoughtful and practical meal plan that aligns with your dietary restrictions and promotes optimal well-being while managing Eosinophilic Esophagitis.

CHAPTER TWO– ANIMAL PROTEIN RECIPES

Embark on a delectable journey into the realm of animal protein recipes, where succulent flavors meet nutritional excellence. From the rich umami of meats to the delicate textures of seafood, these recipes promise not just a feast for the senses but also a powerhouse of essential nutrients. Join us in exploring the art of crafting mouthwatering dishes that celebrate the versatility and nourishing benefits of animal proteins. Whether you're a seasoned chef or an enthusiastic home cook, these recipes are a gateway to culinary adventures that tantalize taste buds and contribute to your overall well-being. Get ready to savor the symphony of flavors that animal proteins bring to the table, turning each meal into a memorable masterpiece.

Baked Chicken Taquitos

Servings: 4 | **Prep Time:** 20 minutes | **Cook Time:** 20 minutes

Ingredients:

- 2 cups shredded cooked chicken (rotisserie chicken works well)

- 1 cup of Mexican blend cheese or even shredded cheddar

- 1/2 cup salsa

- 1/4 cup chopped fresh cilantro

- 1 teaspoon ground cumin

- 1 teaspoon chili powder

- 1/2 teaspoon garlic powder

- 1/2 teaspoon onion powder

- 1/4 teaspoon cayenne pepper (adjust to taste)

- Salt and pepper to taste

- 12 small flour tortillas

- Cooking spray

- Guacamole, sour cream, and salsa for serving

Instructions:

1. Preheat your oven to 425°F (220°C). Line a baking sheet with parchment paper.

2. In a mixing bowl, combine the shredded chicken, shredded cheese, salsa, chopped cilantro, ground cumin, chili powder, garlic powder, onion powder, cayenne pepper, salt, and pepper. Mix until well combined.

3. Place the tortillas between two damp paper towels and microwave for about 20-30 seconds to make them pliable.

4. Spoon a generous amount of the chicken filling onto the lower third of each tortilla. Roll the tortilla tightly around the filling, placing them seam-side down on the prepared baking sheet.

5. Lightly spray the taquitos with cooking spray. Until the edges are golden brown and crispy, bake in the preheated oven for 15-20 minutes or

6. Remove the taquitos from the oven and let them cool slightly. Serve with your favorite sides such as guacamole, sour cream, and extra salsa.

7. **Optional:** Feel free to customize the filling with ingredients like diced green chilies, black beans, or corn for added flavor and texture.

8. Note: These baked chicken taquitos are great for making ahead. Prepare and roll them, then refrigerate until ready to bake.

Enjoy these baked chicken taquitos as a delightful appetizer, snack, or even as a main course. The combination of crispy tortillas and flavorful, cheesy chicken filling is sure to be a crowd-pleaser.

Bacon Ramen Noodles

Servings: 2 | **Prep Time:** 10 minutes | **Cook Time:** 15 minutes

Ingredients:

- 2 packs of ramen noodles

- 4 slices of bacon, chopped

- 1 small onion, finely chopped

- 2 cloves garlic, minced

- 1 carrot, julienned

- 2 cups broccoli florets

- 2 tablespoons mushroom broth

- 1 tablespoon oyster sauce

- 1 teaspoon sesame oil

- 1 thinly sliced green onions (for garnish)

- Sesame seeds (optional, for garnish)

Instructions:

1. Bring a pot of water to a boil and cook the ramen noodles according to the package instructions. Drain and set aside.

2. In a large skillet or wok, cook the chopped bacon over medium heat until it becomes crispy. Remove excess fat if needed.

3. Add chopped onions to the skillet and sauté until they become translucent.

4. Stir in minced garlic, julienned carrots, and broccoli florets. Cook for a few minutes until the vegetables are slightly tender but still vibrant.

5. Add the cooked ramen noodles to the skillet, tossing them with the vegetables and bacon.

6. In a small bowl, mix together the mushroom broth, oyster sauce, and sesame oil. Toss everything

together until well coated that is after pouring the broth over the noodles.

7. Cook for an additional 2-3 minutes, allowing the flavors to meld and the noodles to absorb the sauce.

8. If desired, garnish with sliced green onions and sesame seeds.

9. Serve immediately and enjoy your delicious Bacon Ramen Noodles!

By adding your favorite vegetables or adjusting the sauce to your taste, feel free to customize this recipe. It's a quick and flavorful way to elevate your ramen noodles with the savory goodness of bacon!

Italian Pork Sliders

Servings: 4 | **Prep Time:** 15 minutes | **Cook Time:** 20 minutes

Ingredients:

For the Pork Patties:

- 1 pound of ground pork

- 1/2 cup breadcrumbs

- 1/4 cup grated Parmesan cheese

- 1/4 cup chopped fresh parsley

- 2 cloves garlic, minced

- 1 teaspoon dried oregano

- 1 teaspoon dried basil

- Salt and black pepper to taste

For the Pesto Mayonnaise:

- 1/2 cup mayonnaise

- 2 tablespoons prepared basil pesto

For the Sliders:

- Slider buns

- Sliced fresh mozzarella cheese

- Fresh basil leaves

- Tomato slices

Instructions:

1. To medium heat, preheat your grill or stovetop griddle.

2. In a large bowl, combine ground pork, breadcrumbs, Parmesan cheese, chopped parsley, minced garlic, dried oregano, dried basil, salt, and black pepper. Mix until well combined. Shape the mixture into small slider-sized patties.

3. Grill the pork patties for about 4-5 minutes per side or until fully cooked and nicely charred on the outside.

4. In a small bowl, mix together mayonnaise and basil pesto to create the pesto mayonnaise.

5. Slice the slider buns in half. Spread a generous amount of pesto mayonnaise on the bottom half of each bun. Place a grilled pork patty on each bun. Top with a slice of fresh mozzarella, fresh basil leaves, and a tomato slice. With the top half of the slider bun, cover.

6. Secure each slider with a toothpick if needed, and serve immediately.

7. **Optional:** Consider adding extras like arugula, roasted red peppers, or balsamic glaze for additional flavor.

8. These Italian Pork Sliders pair well with a side of crispy fries or a fresh salad.

Enjoy these Italian-inspired pork sliders as a delightful and flavorful addition to your summer grilling menu or any casual gathering. The combination of seasoned pork, fresh herbs, and savory pesto mayo creates a taste of Italy in every bite.

Apple Sausages Stuffed Butternut Squash

Servings: 4 | **Prep Time:** 15 minutes | **Cook Time:** 45 minutes

Ingredients:

- 2 medium halved and seeds removed of butternut squashes

- 4 apple sausages, casings removed and crumbled

- 1 tablespoon olive oil

- 1 onion, finely chopped

- 2 cloves garlic, minced

- 1 apple, diced

- 1/2 cup dried cranberries

- 1/2 cup chopped pecans

- 1 teaspoon dried sage

- Salt and black pepper to taste

- Fresh parsley, chopped (for garnish)

Instructions:

1. Preheat your oven to 375°F (190°C).

2. Place the halved butternut squashes on a baking sheet, cut side up.

3. In a skillet over medium heat, add olive oil. Sauté until softened after adding chopped onions.

4. Add crumbled apple sausages to the skillet and cook until browned.

5. Stir in minced garlic, diced apple, dried cranberries, chopped pecans, dried sage, salt, and

black pepper. For an additional 3-4 minutes, cook until the ingredients are thoroughly combined.

6. Spoon the sausage and apple mixture evenly into the hollowed-out sections of the butternut squashes.

7. Cover the baking sheet with foil and bake for 30 minutes. Remove the foil and bake for an additional 15 minutes or until the butternut squash is tender and easily pierced with a fork.

8. Garnish with fresh parsley before serving.

9. Serve the stuffed butternut squash halves as a delightful autumn-inspired dish.

Enjoy this hearty and flavorful Apple Sausages Stuffed Butternut Squash as a comforting main course, perfect for fall or any time you crave a wholesome, delicious meal.

Asian Chicken Meatballs

Servings: 4 | **Prep Time:** 15 minutes | **Cook Time:** 20 minutes

Ingredients:

For the Meatballs:

- 1 of pound ground chicken

- 1/2 cup breadcrumbs

- 1/4 cup finely chopped green onions

- 2 cloves garlic, minced

- 1 tablespoon soy sauce

- 1 tablespoon hoisin sauce

- 1 teaspoon sesame oil

- 1 teaspoon grated ginger

- 1 egg, beaten

- Salt and pepper to taste

For the Sauce:

- 1/4 cup soy balsamic vinegar

- 2 tablespoons hoisin sauce

- 1 tablespoon rice vinegar

- 1 tablespoon honey

- 1 teaspoon sesame oil

- 1 teaspoon grated ginger

For Garnish:

- Sesame seeds

- Chopped green onions

- Fresh cilantro, chopped

Instructions:

1. Preheat your oven to 375°F (190°C). Line a baking sheet with parchment paper.

2. In a large bowl, combine ground chicken, breadcrumbs, chopped green onions, minced garlic, balsamic vinegar, hoisin sauce, sesame oil, grated ginger, beaten egg, salt, and pepper. Mix until well combined.

3. Shape the mixture into small meatballs, about 1 inch in diameter, and place them on the prepared baking sheet.

4. Bake the meatballs in the preheated oven for 15-20 minutes or until they are cooked through and golden brown.

5. While the meatballs are baking, prepare the sauce. In a small saucepan, combine soy sauce, hoisin sauce, rice vinegar, honey, sesame oil, and grated ginger. Until the sauce thickens slightly, simmer over low heat

6. Once the meatballs are done, brush them generously with the Asian sauce.

7. Garnish the meatballs with sesame seeds, chopped green onions, and fresh cilantro.

8. Serve the Asian Chicken Meatballs as an appetizer or as a main dish over rice or noodles.

Enjoy these flavorful Asian Chicken Meatballs with their sweet and savory glaze—a perfect addition to your Asian-inspired culinary repertoire.

Paprika Chicken Drumsticks

Servings: 4 | **Prep Time:** 10 minutes | **Cook Time:** 40 minutes

Ingredients:

- 8 chicken drumsticks

- 2 tablespoons olive oil

- 2 teaspoons smoked paprika

- 1 teaspoon sweet paprika

- 1 teaspoon garlic powder

- 1 teaspoon onion powder

- 1 teaspoon dried thyme

- 1 teaspoon dried oregano

- 1/2 teaspoon cayenne pepper (adjust to taste)

- Salt and black pepper to taste

- Fresh parsley, chopped (for garnish)

Instructions:

1. Preheat your oven to 400°F (200°C). Line a baking sheet with parchment paper.

2. In a small bowl, mix together smoked paprika, sweet paprika, garlic powder, onion powder, dried thyme, dried oregano, cayenne pepper, salt, and black pepper.

3. Pat the chicken drumsticks dry with a paper towel. Rub the spice mixture evenly over each drumstick.

4. Drizzle olive oil over the drumsticks and toss to coat them evenly in the spice mixture.

5. Arrange the drumsticks on the prepared baking sheet.

6. Bake in the preheated oven for 35-40 minutes or until the drumsticks are golden brown and the internal temperature reaches 165°F (74°C).

7. Before serving, garnish with chopped fresh parsley.

8. Serve the Paprika Chicken Drumsticks hot as a flavorful and spicy main dish.

Enjoy these Paprika Chicken Drumsticks for a simple yet delicious meal that's rich in warm, smoky flavors.

Beef and Quinoa Meatballs

Servings: 4 | **Prep Time:** 15 minutes | **Cook Time:** 25 minutes

Ingredients:

For the Meatballs:

- 1 of pound ground beef

- 1 cup cooked quinoa, cooled

- 1/2 cup breadcrumbs

- 1/4 cup grated Parmesan cheese

- 1/4 cup chopped fresh parsley

- 2 cloves garlic, minced

- 1 teaspoon dried oregano

- Salt and black pepper to taste

- Olive oil for cooking

For the Tomato Sauce:

- 1 can (14 oz) crushed tomatoes

- 2 cloves garlic, minced

- 1 teaspoon dried basil

- 1 teaspoon dried oregano

- Salt and black pepper to taste

Instructions:

1. Preheat your oven to 375°F (190°C).

2. In a large mixing bowl, combine ground beef, cooked quinoa, breadcrumbs, grated Parmesan cheese, chopped fresh parsley, minced garlic, dried oregano, salt, and black pepper. Mix until well combined.

3. Approximately 1 inch in diameter, shape the mixture into meatballs,

4. Over medium heat, heat the olive oil in a skillet. Brown the meatballs on all sides, working in batches if needed.

5. In a separate saucepan, combine crushed tomatoes, minced garlic, dried basil, dried oregano, salt, and black pepper. For 10-15 minutes, stirring occasionally, simmer over low heat

6. Transfer the browned meatballs to a baking dish and cover them with the tomato sauce.

7. Bake in the preheated oven for 20-25 minutes or until the meatballs are cooked through.

8. Serve the Beef and Quinoa Meatballs over cooked quinoa or your favorite pasta.

Enjoy these hearty and flavorful Beef and Quinoa Meatballs as a wholesome meal, perfect for a family dinner or a comforting weeknight dish.

Sausage and Peppers Pasta

Servings: 4 | **Prep Time:** 15 minutes | **Cook Time:** 25 minutes

Ingredients:

- 8 ounces (about 225g) penne or your favorite pasta

- 1 pound (about 450g) Italian sausage, sliced

- 2 tablespoons olive oil

- 1 onion, thinly sliced

- 2 bell peppers (any color), thinly sliced

- 3 cloves garlic, minced

- 1 can (14 oz) crushed tomatoes

- 1 teaspoon dried oregano

- 1 teaspoon dried basil

- Salt and black pepper to taste

- Red pepper flakes (optional, for heat)

- Chopped Fresh basil or parsley for extra garnish

- Grated Parmesan cheese (for serving)

Instructions:

1. According to the package instructions, cook the pasta. Drain and set aside.

2. In a large skillet, heat olive oil over medium-high heat. Add sliced Italian sausage and cook until browned on both sides. From the skillet, remove the sausage and set aside.

3. In the same skillet, add sliced onion and bell peppers. Sauté until softened.

4. Add minced garlic and sauté for an additional minute until fragrant.

5. Pour in crushed tomatoes, dried oregano, dried basil, salt, black pepper, and red pepper flakes if using. Stir to combine.

6. Return the cooked sausage to the skillet. Allowing the flavors to meld, simmer the mixture for 10-15 minutes.

7. Toss the cooked pasta into the skillet, ensuring it's well coated in the sausage and peppers mixture.

8. Garnish with chopped fresh basil or parsley.

9. Serve the Sausage and Peppers Pasta hot, with grated Parmesan cheese on top.

Enjoy this flavorful and satisfying Sausage and Peppers Pasta as a comforting and easy-to-make dish for any occasion.

Creamy Lemon Chicken Pasta

Servings: 4 | **Prep Time:** 15 minutes | **Cook Time:** 20 minutes

Ingredients:

- 8 ounces (about 225g) fettuccine or your preferred pasta

- 2 boneless, skinless chicken breasts, thinly sliced

- Salt and black pepper to taste

- 2 tablespoons olive oil

- 3 cloves garlic, minced

- 1 cup cherry tomatoes, halved

- 1 cup baby spinach leaves

- 1 cup heavy cream

- Zest of 1 lemon

- Juice of 1 lemon

- 1/2 cup grated Parmesan cheese

- Fresh parsley, chopped (for garnish)

Instructions:

1. According to the package instructions. cook the pasta Drain and set aside.

2. Season the sliced chicken breasts with salt and black pepper.

3. In a large skillet, heat olive oil over medium-high heat. Add the seasoned chicken slices and cook until browned on both sides and fully cooked. From the skillet remove the chicken and set aside.

4. Add minced garlic and sauté for about 1 minute until fragrant, in the same skillet.

5. Add halved cherry tomatoes to the skillet and cook until they start to soften.

6. Stir in baby spinach leaves and cook until wilted.

7. Pour in the heavy cream, lemon zest, and lemon juice. Stir to combine.

8. Add the cooked pasta to the skillet, tossing to coat it in the creamy lemon sauce.

9. Return the cooked chicken slices to the skillet. Sprinkle grated Parmesan cheese over the mixture and gently stir.

10. Garnish with chopped fresh parsley.

11. Serve the Creamy Lemon Chicken Pasta hot, with an extra sprinkle of Parmesan cheese if desired.

Enjoy this delightful Creamy Lemon Chicken Pasta, where the zesty lemon flavors perfectly complement the richness of the creamy sauce, creating a deliciously comforting meal.

San Francisco Pork Chops

Servings: 4 | **Prep Time:** 15 minutes | **Cook Time:** 25 minutes

Ingredients:

- 4 bone-in pork chops

- Salt and black pepper to taste

- 2 tablespoons olive oil

- 1 onion, thinly sliced

- 1 bell pepper (any color), thinly sliced

- 2 cloves garlic, minced

- 1 can of diced and drained tomatoes (14 oz)

- 1/2 cup chicken broth

- 1 teaspoon dried oregano

- 1 teaspoon dried basil

- 1 teaspoon smoked paprika

- 1/2 teaspoon of red pepper flakes, it is completely optional for heat

- Fresh parsley, chopped (for garnish)

Instructions:

1. Season pork chops with salt and black pepper on both sides.

2. In a large skillet, heat olive oil over medium-high heat. Add pork chops and sear until browned on both sides. Set aside and remove chops from the skillet.

3. In the same skillet, add sliced onion and bell pepper. Sauté until softened.

4. Add minced garlic and sauté for an additional minute until fragrant.

5. Pour in diced tomatoes, chicken broth, dried oregano, dried basil, smoked paprika, and red pepper flakes if using. Stir to combine.

6. Return the seared pork chops to the skillet, nestling them into the vegetable mixture.

7. Simmer over medium heat for 15-20 minutes or until the pork chops are cooked through and tender.

8. Garnish with chopped fresh parsley.

9. Serve the San Francisco Pork Chops hot, over rice or your favorite side.

Enjoy these flavorful San Francisco Pork Chops, where the combination of tomatoes, peppers, and aromatic spices creates a savory and satisfying dish reminiscent of the iconic flavors of San Francisco cuisine.

CHAPTER THREE– GRAINS RECIPES

Embark on a journey into the heart of wholesome and diverse flavors with our collection of grain-based recipes. Grains, the cornerstone of countless cuisines worldwide, offer a canvas for culinary creativity. From the nutty aroma of quinoa to the comforting familiarity of rice and the hearty texture of pasta, each grain brings a unique character to your plate. In this culinary exploration, discover a spectrum of recipes that showcase the versatility of grains. Whether you seek the comfort of a warm bowl of risotto, the vibrant colors of a grain salad, or the satisfying crunch of a quinoa bowl, our collection has something for every palate and occasion. Join us as we elevate simple grains into extraordinary dishes, celebrating their rich history and inviting you to savor the diverse, nutritious, and delicious world of grain-based cuisine. Get ready to embrace a symphony of textures and flavors that will tantalize your taste buds and bring a wholesome, hearty goodness to your table. Welcome to the wonderful realm of grain recipes—a journey of taste and nourishment awaits!

One Pan Mexican Mince and Rice

Servings: 4 | **Prep Time:** 15 minutes | **Cook Time:** 30 minutes

Ingredients:

- 1 pound of (about 450g) ground beef or turkey

- 1 cup long-grain rice

- 1 onion, finely chopped

- 1 bell pepper (any color), diced

- 1 can (14 oz) black beans, drained and rinsed

- 1 cup corn kernels (fresh or frozen)

- 1 can (14 oz) diced tomatoes with green chilies

- 2 cups chicken broth

- 2 teaspoons ground cumin

- 1 teaspoon chili powder

- 1 teaspoon smoked paprika

- Salt and black pepper to taste

- Fresh cilantro, chopped (for garnish)

- Lime wedges (for serving)

Instructions:

1. In a large skillet or pan, brown the ground beef or turkey over medium-high heat. Drain excess fat if needed.

2. Add chopped onion and diced bell pepper to the skillet. Sauté until the vegetables are softened.

3. Stir in long-grain rice, black beans, corn, diced tomatoes with green chilies, chicken broth, ground cumin, chili powder, smoked paprika, salt, and black pepper. Mix well.

4. Reduce the heat to low after bringing the mixture to Cover the pan and let it simmer for 20-25 minutes or until the rice is cooked and the liquid is absorbed.

5. Once cooked, fluff the rice with a fork and ensure everything is well combined.

6. Garnish with chopped fresh cilantro.

7. Serve the One Pan Mexican Mince and Rice hot, with lime wedges on the side for a burst of citrus freshness.

Enjoy this easy and flavorful one-pan meal that brings the vibrant and robust flavors of Mexican cuisine to your table with the convenience of minimal cleanup.

Baked Honey Mustard Chicken and Potatoes

Servings: 4 | **Prep Time:** 15 minutes | **Cook Time:** 45 minutes

Ingredients:

- 4 bone-in, skin-on chicken thighs

- 4 medium-sized potatoes, washed and cut into chunks

- 2 tablespoons olive oil

- Salt and black pepper to taste

- 2 tablespoons whole grain mustard

- 2 tablespoons honey

- 2 cloves garlic, minced

- 1 tablespoon fresh rosemary, chopped

- 1 tablespoon fresh thyme leaves

Instructions:

1. Preheat your oven to 400°F (200°C). Grease a baking dish with olive oil or non-stick cooking spray.

2. Season chicken thighs and potato chunks with salt and black pepper.

3. In a small bowl, whisk together whole grain mustard, honey, minced garlic, chopped rosemary, and thyme leaves.

4. Place chicken thighs and potato chunks in the prepared baking dish.

5. Drizzle olive oil over the chicken and potatoes. Toss to coat evenly.

6. Pour the honey mustard mixture over the chicken and potatoes, ensuring they are well coated.

7. Arrange the chicken thighs skin-side up in the baking dish, with the potatoes around them.

8. Bake in the preheated oven for 40-45 minutes or until the chicken is cooked through and the potatoes are tender, with crispy edges.

9. Once baked, remove from the oven and let it rest for a few minutes.

10. Serve the Baked Honey Mustard Chicken and Potatoes hot, garnished with additional chopped fresh herbs if desired.

Enjoy this delicious and easy-to-make Baked Honey Mustard Chicken and Potatoes recipe, where tender chicken thighs and golden potatoes are coated in a sweet and tangy glaze, making it a comforting and satisfying meal for any occasion.

Strawberry Quinoa Salad with Feta

Servings: 4 | **Prep Time:** 15 minutes | **Cook Time:** 20 minutes

Ingredients:

- 1 cup quinoa, rinsed

- 2 cups water

- 1 pint of hulled and sliced fresh strawberries,

- 1/2 cup crumbled feta cheese

- 1/4 cup chopped fresh mint leaves

- 1/4 cup chopped fresh basil leaves

- 1/4 cup sliced almonds

- 2 tablespoons extra virgin olive oil

- 2 tablespoons balsamic vinegar

- Salt and black pepper to taste

Instructions:

1. Bring water to a boil in a medium saucepan. Add quinoa, reduce heat to low, cover, and simmer for 15-20 minutes or until quinoa is tender and water is absorbed. Allow to cool after removing from heat.

2. In a large mixing bowl, combine cooked quinoa, sliced strawberries, crumbled feta cheese, chopped mint leaves, chopped basil leaves, and sliced almonds.

3. In a small bowl, whisk together extra virgin olive oil and balsamic vinegar. To taste season with salt and black pepper.

4. Drizzle the dressing over the salad and toss gently to combine, ensuring all ingredients are evenly coated.

5. Serve the Strawberry Quinoa Salad with Feta chilled or at room temperature.

Enjoy this refreshing and flavorful Strawberry Quinoa Salad with Feta, where the sweetness of strawberries and the creaminess of feta cheese perfectly complement the nutty texture of quinoa, creating a balance of flavors and textures in every bite that you take.

Slow Cooker Pork Tacos

Servings: 4 | **Prep Time:** 15 minutes | **Cook Time:** 6-8 hours (Slow Cooker)

Ingredients:

- 2 pounds pork shoulder or pork butt, trimmed of excess fat

- 1 tablespoon chili powder

- 1 teaspoon ground cumin

- 1 teaspoon smoked paprika

- 1 teaspoon garlic powder

- 1 teaspoon onion powder

- 1/2 teaspoon dried oregano

- 1/2 teaspoon salt

- 1/4 teaspoon black pepper

- 1 cup chicken broth

- 1/4 cup lime juice

- Corn or flour tortillas, for serving

- Your favorite taco toppings (salsa, shredded lettuce, diced tomatoes, diced onions, avocado slices, etc.)

Instructions:

1. In a small bowl, mix together chili powder, ground cumin, smoked paprika, garlic powder, onion powder, dried oregano, salt, and black pepper to create the taco seasoning.

2. Rub the taco seasoning all over the pork shoulder or pork butt.

3. In a slow cooker, place the already seasoned pork.

4. Pour chicken broth and lime juice over the pork.

5. Cover and cook on low for 6-8 hours or on high for 3-4 hours, until the pork is tender and easily shreds with a fork.

6. Once cooked, remove the pork from the slow cooker and shred it using two forks. Remove any excess fat if desired.

7. Return the shredded pork to the slow cooker and toss it in the juices to coat.

8. Warm the tortillas according to package instructions.

9. Assemble the tacos by placing a generous amount of shredded pork onto each tortilla and topping with your favorite taco toppings.

10. Serve the Slow Cooker Pork Tacos hot and enjoy the delicious and flavorful meal!

These Slow Cooker Pork Tacos are incredibly tender and bursting with savory flavors, making them perfect for a delicious weeknight dinner or for entertaining guests. Enjoy the convenience of your slow cooker while savoring the authentic taste of homemade tacos.

Salsa Chicken Sheet Pan

Servings: 4 | **Prep Time:** 10 minutes | **Cook Time:** 25 minutes

Ingredients:

- 4 boneless, skinless chicken breasts

- Salt and black pepper, to taste

- 1 teaspoon chili powder

- 1 teaspoon ground cumin

- 1 teaspoon garlic powder

- 1 teaspoon onion powder

- 1 cup salsa

- 1 cup shredded cheddar cheese

- 1 avocado, sliced (optional, for serving)

- Fresh cilantro, chopped (optional, for garnish)

Instructions:

1. Preheat your oven to 400°F (200°C). For easy cleanup, line a baking sheet with parchment paper or even aluminum foil depending on what is available.

2. Place the chicken breasts on the prepared baking sheet and season both sides with salt and black pepper.

3. In a small bowl, mix together chili powder, ground cumin, garlic powder, and onion powder. Over the chicken breasts, evenly sprinkle the spice mixture.

4. Spoon salsa over each chicken breast, spreading it to cover the surface.

5. Transfer the baking sheet to the preheated oven and bake for 20-25 minutes, or until the chicken is cooked through and reaches an internal temperature of 165°F (75°C).

6. Remove the baking sheet from the oven and sprinkle shredded cheddar cheese over each chicken breast.

7. Return the baking sheet to the oven and bake for an additional 3-5 minutes, or until the cheese is melted and bubbly.

8. Remove from the oven and let the chicken rest for a few minutes before serving.

9. Serve the Salsa Chicken hot, garnished with sliced avocado and chopped cilantro if desired.

Enjoy this easy and flavorful Salsa Chicken Sheet Pan recipe, where juicy chicken breasts are topped with tangy salsa and melted cheddar cheese for a deliciously satisfying meal that's ready in no time!

Lemon Chicken Pasta

Servings: 4 | **Prep Time:** 10 minutes | **Cook Time:** 20 minutes

Ingredients:

- 8 ounces (about 225g) linguine or your favorite pasta

- 2 boneless, skinless chicken breasts, thinly sliced

- Salt and black pepper, to taste

- 2 tablespoons olive oil

- 3 cloves garlic, minced

- Zest of 1 lemon

- Juice of 1 lemon

- 1 cup cherry tomatoes, halved

- 1/2 cup chicken broth

- 1/4 cup heavy cream

- 1/4 cup grated Parmesan cheese

- 2 tablespoons chopped fresh parsley

Instructions:

1. According to the package instructions, cook the pasta. Drain and set aside, reserve about 1/2 cup of the pasta water.

2. Season the sliced chicken breasts with salt and black pepper.

3. Heat olive oil over medium-high heat, In a large skillet. Add the seasoned chicken slices you already have and cook until you see that it is browned on both sides and cooked through. Set aside after removing the chicken from the skillet.

4. In the same skillet, add minced garlic and sauté for about 1 minute until fragrant.

5. Add lemon zest and lemon juice to the skillet, stirring to deglaze the pan.

6. Stir in halved cherry tomatoes and cook until they start to soften.

7. Pour in chicken broth and heavy cream, stirring to combine. Let the mixture simmer for a few minutes to reduce slightly.

8. Add cooked pasta to the skillet, tossing to coat it in the lemon sauce. If the sauce seems too thick, add some of the reserved pasta water to reach your desired consistency.

9. Return the cooked chicken slices to the skillet, mixing them with the pasta and sauce.

10. Sprinkle grated Parmesan cheese over the mixture and toss to combine.

11. With chopped fresh parsley, garnish before serving.

12. Serve the Lemon Chicken Pasta hot, with additional Parmesan cheese and lemon wedges on the side if desired.

Enjoy this delightful Lemon Chicken Pasta, where the bright citrus flavors perfectly complement the tender chicken and creamy sauce, creating a refreshing and satisfying meal for any occasion!

Apple Cinnamon Brown Rice Breakfast Bake

Servings: 6 | **Prep Time:** 15 minutes | **Cook Time:** 40 minutes

Ingredients:

- 1 cup brown rice, rinsed

- 2 cups of unsweetened almond milk (or any preferred milk of your choice depending on what you have

- 2 large apples, peeled and diced

- 1/4 cup pure maple syrup

- 1 teaspoon ground cinnamon

- 1/2 teaspoon ground nutmeg

- 1/4 teaspoon ground ginger

- 1/4 teaspoon salt

- 1/2 cup chopped pecans (optional, for topping)

- Greek yogurt or additional maple syrup, for serving (optional)

Instructions:

1. Preheat your oven to 375°F (190°C). With cooking spray or butter grease a 9x9 inch baking dish.

2. In a medium saucepan, combine brown rice and almond milk. Bring to a boil over medium heat, then reduce heat to low, cover, and simmer for 15-20 minutes or until quinoa is cooked and liquid is absorbed.

3. While the brown rice is cooking, in a large bowl, toss diced apples with maple syrup, ground cinnamon, ground nutmeg, ground ginger, and salt until well coated.

4. Once the brown rice is cooked, add it to the bowl with the apples and stir until evenly combined.

5. Transfer the brown rice and apple mixture to the prepared baking dish, spreading it out evenly.

6. If using chopped pecans, sprinkle them evenly over the top of the brown rice and apple mixture.

7. Bake in the preheated oven for 20-25 minutes or until the edges are golden brown and the mixture is set.

8. Remove from the oven and let it cool slightly before serving.

9. Serve the Apple Cinnamon Brown rice Breakfast Bake warm, topped with Greek yogurt or an additional drizzle of maple syrup if desired.

Enjoy this wholesome and flavorful Apple Cinnamon Brown Rice Breakfast Bake, where the comforting combination of apples, cinnamon, and nutmeg creates a deliciously satisfying breakfast or brunch option that's perfect for starting your day on a sweet note!

Avocado and Garbanzo Bean Cauliflower Rice Salad

Servings: 4 | **Prep Time:** 15 minutes | **Cook Time:** 15 minutes

Ingredients:

- 1 cup cauliflower rice, rinsed

- 2 cups water or vegetable broth

- 1 can of drained and rinsed (15 oz) of garbanzo beans (also known as chickpeas)

- 1 ripe avocado, diced

- 1 cup cherry tomatoes, halved

- 1/2 cup cucumber, diced

- 1/4 cup red onion, finely chopped

- 1/4 cup fresh cilantro, chopped

- 1/4 cup fresh parsley, chopped

- Juice of 1 lime

- 2 tablespoons extra virgin olive oil

- 1 clove garlic, minced

- Salt and black pepper, to taste

Instructions:

1. In a medium saucepan, combine cauliflower rice and water or vegetable broth. Bring to a boil over medium heat, then reduce heat to low, cover, and simmer for 15 minutes or until the cauliflower rice is cooked and liquid is absorbed. Remove off from heat and allow it to cool.

2. In a large mixing bowl, combine cooked cauliflower rice, garbanzo beans, diced avocado, cherry tomatoes, diced cucumber, finely chopped red onion, chopped cilantro, and chopped parsley.

3. In a small bowl, whisk together lime juice, extra virgin olive oil, minced garlic, salt, and black pepper.

4. Pour the dressing over the cauliflower rice salad and toss gently to combine, ensuring all ingredients are evenly coated.

5. Taste and adjust seasoning if needed.

6. Serve the Avocado and Garbanzo Bean Cauliflower Rice Salad chilled or at room temperature.

Enjoy this refreshing and nutritious Avocado and Garbanzo Bean Cauliflower Rice Salad, where creamy avocado, protein-rich garbanzo beans, and flavorful herbs come together with quinoa for a satisfying and delicious dish that's perfect for lunch, dinner, or as a side at your next gathering!

Cherry Pecan Granola with Quinoa

Servings: About 8 cups | **Prep Time:** 10 minutes | **Cook Time:** 25 minutes

Ingredients:

- 3 cups old-fashioned rolled oats

- 1 cup uncooked quinoa, rinsed

- 1 cup pecans, chopped

- 1/2 cup unsweetened shredded coconut

- 1/2 cup dried cherries, chopped

- 1/4 cup maple syrup

- 1/4 cup coconut oil, melted

- 1 teaspoon vanilla extract

- 1/2 teaspoon ground cinnamon

- 1/4 teaspoon salt

Instructions:

1. Preheat your oven to 325°F (160°C). Using parchment paper, carefully line a large baking sheet.

2. In a large mixing bowl, combine rolled oats, rinsed quinoa, chopped pecans, shredded coconut, and dried cherries. Mix well.

3. In a separate small bowl, whisk together maple syrup, melted coconut oil, vanilla extract, ground cinnamon, and salt until well combined.

4. Pour the wet ingredients over the dry ingredients in the large mixing bowl. Stir until everything is evenly coated.

5. Spread the granola mixture in an even layer on the prepared baking sheet.

6. Bake in the preheated oven for 20-25 minutes, stirring halfway through, or until the granola is golden brown and fragrant.

7. After removing from the oven allow the granola to cool completely on the baking sheet. As it cools further, it will continue to crisp

8. Once cooled, break the granola into clusters and store it in an airtight container at room temperature for up to two weeks.

9. Serve the Cherry Pecan Granola with Quinoa as a topping for yogurt, as a crunchy cereal with milk, or as a snack on its own.

Enjoy this homemade Cherry Pecan Granola with Quinoa, where the combination of oats, quinoa, pecans, coconut, and dried cherries creates a deliciously crunchy and nutritious treat that's perfect for breakfast or anytime snacking!

Quinoa Porridge

Servings: 4 | **Prep Time:** 5 minutes | **Cook Time:** 20 minutes

Ingredients:

- 1 cup quinoa, rinsed

- 2 cups water or milk (almond milk, coconut milk, or dairy milk)

- 1/4 teaspoon salt

- 2 tablespoons honey or maple syrup (optional)

- 1 teaspoon ground cinnamon

- 1/2 teaspoon vanilla extract

- Toppings of your choice: sliced bananas, berries, chopped nuts, seeds, dried fruits, coconut flakes, etc.

Instructions:

1. In a fine mesh sieve, rinse the quinoa under cold water for about 1 minute to remove any bitterness.

2. In a medium saucepan, combine the rinsed quinoa, water or milk, and salt. Over medium-high heat, Bring to a boil.

3. Once boiling, reduce the heat to low and cover the saucepan with a lid. Simmer for 15-20 minutes, or until the quinoa is cooked and the liquid is absorbed. Stir occasionally to prevent sticking.

4. Once the quinoa is cooked, remove the saucepan from the heat. If desired, stir in honey or maple syrup, ground cinnamon, and vanilla extract for added sweetness and flavor.

5. Serve the quinoa porridge warm in bowls.

6. Top with your favorite toppings such as sliced bananas, berries, chopped nuts, seeds, dried fruits, or coconut flakes.

7. Enjoy this nutritious and satisfying Quinoa Porridge as a wholesome breakfast or snack.

This Quinoa Porridge is a delicious and versatile alternative to traditional oatmeal, offering a boost of protein and fiber to start your day right. Customize it with your favorite toppings for a nourishing and flavorful meal that will keep you feeling satisfied and energized!

CHAPTER THREE– VEGETABLES AND LEAFY GREENS

Vegetables and leafy greens are nature's gift, offering a symphony of colors, flavors, and nutrients. From the crisp crunch of fresh carrots to the delicate bite of spinach, these vibrant ingredients form the foundation of a healthy and nourishing diet. Packed with vitamins, minerals, and antioxidants, vegetables and leafy greens not only tantalize the taste buds but also promote vitality and well-being. Join us on a journey to explore the endless possibilities of incorporating these wholesome treasures into your culinary repertoire, unlocking a world of culinary creativity and vibrant health.

Kale and Apple Salad

Servings: 4 | **Prep Time:** 10 minutes

Ingredients:

- 1 bunch kale, stems removed and leaves thinly sliced

- 1 large apple, thinly sliced

- 1/4 cup dried cranberries

- 1/4 cup chopped pecans or walnuts

- 1/4 cup crumbled feta cheese (optional)

- 2 tablespoons lemon juice

- 2 tablespoons extra virgin olive oil

- 1 tablespoon honey or maple syrup

- Salt and black pepper, to taste

Instructions:

1. In a large mixing bowl, combine the thinly sliced kale leaves, apple slices, dried cranberries, chopped pecans or walnuts, and crumbled feta cheese (if using).

2. In a small bowl, whisk together the lemon juice, extra virgin olive oil, honey or maple syrup, salt, and black pepper to make the dressing.

3. Pour the dressing over the salad ingredients in the large mixing bowl.

4. Using clean hands, gently massage the kale leaves with the dressing for about 1-2 minutes. This helps to tenderize the kale and infuse it with flavor.

5. Once the kale is well coated with the dressing and has softened slightly, taste the salad and adjust the seasoning if needed.

6. Transfer the kale and apple salad to a serving dish or divide it among individual plates.

7. Serve immediately as a refreshing side dish or light meal.

Enjoy the crisp and refreshing flavors of this Kale and Apple Salad, where the combination of sweet apples, tart cranberries, crunchy nuts, and tangy dressing perfectly complements the hearty texture of kale, creating a delightful harmony of taste and texture!

Cabbage and Pineapple Stir-Fry

Servings: 4 | **Prep Time:** 10 minutes | **Cook Time:** 10 minutes

Ingredients:

- 1/2 small cabbage, thinly sliced

- 1 cup of fresh or canned pineapple chunks

- 1 red bell pepper, thinly sliced

- 1 small onion, thinly sliced

- 2 cloves garlic, minced

- 1 tablespoon grated ginger

- 2 tablespoons balsamic vinegar

- 1 tablespoon rice vinegar

- 1 tablespoon honey or maple syrup

- 1 tablespoon sesame oil

- 2 tablespoons vegetable oil

- Salt and black pepper, to taste

- For garnish which is completely optional, use chopped green onions, sesame seeds

Instructions:

1. Over medium-high heat, heat vegetable oil in a large skillet or wok

2. Add minced garlic and grated ginger to the skillet. Stir-fry for about 30 seconds until fragrant.

3. Add thinly sliced onion and red bell pepper to the skillet. Stir-fry for 2-3 minutes until slightly softened.

4. Add thinly sliced cabbage to the skillet. Stir-fry for an additional 2-3 minutes until cabbage begins to wilt but still retains some crunch.

5. In a small bowl, mix together balsamic vinegar, rice vinegar, honey or maple syrup, and sesame oil to make the sauce.

6. Pour the sauce over the cabbage and vegetable mixture in the skillet. Stir well to coat everything evenly.

7. Add pineapple chunks to the skillet and toss to combine.

8. Cook for another 1-2 minutes until the pineapple is heated through.

9. To taste, season with salt and black pepper.

10. Remove from heat and transfer the Cabbage and Pineapple Stir-Fry to a serving dish.

11. Garnish with chopped green onions and sesame seeds, if desired.

12. Serve hot as a flavorful and vibrant side dish or over cooked rice or noodles for a complete meal.

Enjoy this delightful Cabbage and Pineapple Stir-Fry, where the sweetness of pineapple pairs perfectly with the savory flavors of cabbage and bell pepper, creating a colorful and satisfying dish that's quick and easy to prepare!

Broccoli and Quinoa Casserole

Servings: 6 | **Prep Time:** 15 minutes | **Cook Time:** 30 minutes

Ingredients:

- 1 cup quinoa, rinsed

- 2 cups vegetable broth or water

- 1 head broccoli, cut into florets

- 1 small onion, diced

- 2 cloves garlic, minced

- 1 cup shredded cheddar cheese

- 1/4 cup grated Parmesan cheese

- 1/2 cup plain Greek yogurt

- 1/4 cup milk (any type)

- 1 tablespoon olive oil

- 1 teaspoon dried thyme

- 1/2 teaspoon dried oregano

- Salt and black pepper, to taste

- Optional topping: breadcrumbs or crushed crackers

Instructions:

1. Preheat your oven to 375°F (190°C). With cooking spray or butter grease a 9x13 inch baking dish.

2. In a medium saucepan, bring vegetable broth or water to a boil. Add quinoa, reduce heat to low, cover, and simmer for 15 minutes or until quinoa is cooked and liquid is absorbed. Allow to cool after you remove from heat.

3. While the quinoa is cooking, steam the broccoli florets until tender. Drain and set aside.

4. Over medium heat, in a large skillet, heat olive oil. Sautéing until softened and fragrant, add diced onion and minced garlic.

5. In a large mixing bowl, combine cooked quinoa, steamed broccoli florets, sautéed onion and garlic mixture, shredded cheddar cheese, grated Parmesan cheese, Greek yogurt, milk, dried thyme, dried oregano, salt, and black pepper. Mix until well combined.

6. Transfer the quinoa and broccoli mixture to the prepared baking dish, spreading it out evenly.

7. If desired, sprinkle breadcrumbs or crushed crackers over the top of the casserole for added crunch.

8. Bake in the preheated oven for 25-30 minutes or until the casserole is heated through and the top is golden brown and bubbly.

9. Remove from the oven and let it cool slightly before serving.

10. Serve the Broccoli and Quinoa Casserole hot as a satisfying and nutritious main dish or side.

Enjoy this comforting and flavorful Broccoli and Quinoa Casserole, where tender quinoa and broccoli are baked to perfection in a creamy and cheesy sauce, making it a wholesome and delicious addition to any meal!

Broccoli Pesto Pasta

Servings: 4 | **Prep Time:** 10 minutes | **Cook Time:** 15 minutes

Ingredients:

- 8 ounces (about 225g) pasta of your choice

- 2 cups broccoli florets

- 2 cloves garlic, minced

- 1/2 cup fresh basil leaves

- 1/4 cup grated Parmesan cheese

- 1/4 cup of toasted pine nuts or even walnuts

- 1/4 cup extra virgin olive oil

- 1 tablespoon fresh lemon juice

- Salt and black pepper, to taste

- Optional garnish: additional grated Parmesan cheese, chopped fresh basil leaves

Instructions:

1. Cook the pasta according to the package instructions in a large pot of salted boiling water. Add the broccoli florets to the boiling water during the last 2-3 minutes of cooking. Drain the pasta and broccoli, reserving about 1/2 cup of pasta water.

2. In a food processor or blender, combine minced garlic, fresh basil leaves, grated Parmesan cheese, toasted pine nuts or walnuts, extra virgin olive oil, and fresh lemon juice. Blend until smooth and well combined. If the pesto is too thick, you can add a little bit of the reserved pasta water to reach your desired consistency.

3. In a large mixing bowl, toss the cooked pasta and broccoli with the prepared pesto sauce until everything is evenly coated. To taste, season with salt and black pepper.

4. Serve the Broccoli Pesto Pasta hot, garnished with additional grated Parmesan cheese and chopped fresh basil leaves if desired.

5. Enjoy this delicious and nutritious Broccoli Pesto Pasta as a satisfying and flavorful meal that's perfect for any occasion!

This Broccoli Pesto Pasta combines tender pasta and vibrant broccoli with a flavorful homemade pesto sauce, creating a delicious and wholesome dish that's sure to please your taste buds!

Broccoli and Avocado Salad

Servings: 4 | **Prep Time:** 10 minutes | **Cook Time:** 0 minutes

Ingredients:

- 2 cups broccoli florets, blanched and cooled

- 1 ripe avocado, diced

- 1/4 cup red onion, finely chopped

- 1/4 cup sunflower seeds

- 2 tablespoons fresh lemon juice

- 2 tablespoons extra virgin olive oil

- 1 tablespoon honey or maple syrup

- 1 teaspoon Dijon mustard

- Salt and black pepper, to taste

- Optional garnish: chopped fresh parsley or cilantro

Instructions:

1. In a large mixing bowl, combine blanched broccoli florets, diced avocado, finely chopped red onion, and sunflower seeds.

2. In a small bowl, whisk together fresh lemon juice, extra virgin olive oil, honey or maple syrup, Dijon mustard, salt, and black pepper to make the dressing.

3. Pour the dressing over the broccoli and avocado mixture in the large mixing bowl. Toss gently to coat everything evenly.

4. Taste the salad and adjust seasoning if needed.

5. Transfer the Broccoli and Avocado Salad to a serving dish.

6. Garnish with chopped fresh parsley or cilantro if desired.

7. Serve immediately as a refreshing and nutritious side dish or light meal.

Enjoy the vibrant flavors and textures of this Broccoli and Avocado Salad, where the creamy avocado perfectly complements the crisp broccoli, creating a delightful harmony of taste and freshness in every bite!

Kale Caesar Salad

Servings: 4 | **Prep Time:** 15 minutes | **Cook Time:** 0 minutes

Ingredients:

- 1 bunch of kale, with the stems removed and the leaves torn into bite-sized pieces

- 1/2 cup of Caesar dressing, it could be store-bought or even homemade

- 1/4 cup grated Parmesan cheese

- 1/2 cup croutons

- 1/4 cup cherry tomatoes, halved (optional)

- Salt and black pepper, to taste

- Lemon wedges, for serving (optional)

Instructions:

1. In a large mixing bowl, add the torn kale leaves.

2. Pour Caesar dressing over the kale leaves. Using clean hands, massage the dressing into the kale leaves for about 2-3 minutes until the kale starts to soften and become tender.

3. Add grated Parmesan cheese to the bowl and toss to combine.

4. Taste the salad and season with salt and black pepper to taste.

5. Add croutons to the salad and toss gently to distribute them evenly.

6. If desired, add halved cherry tomatoes for extra color and flavor.

7. Transfer the Kale Caesar Salad to a serving dish or individual plates.

8. Serve immediately as a refreshing and satisfying side dish or light meal.

9. Garnish with additional grated Parmesan cheese and lemon wedges if desired.

Enjoy the crisp and flavorful goodness of this Kale Caesar Salad, where the hearty kale leaves are coated in creamy Caesar dressing and topped with crunchy croutons, creating a delicious and nutritious salad that's perfect for any occasion!

Cauliflower Rice Pilaf

Servings: 4 | **Prep Time:** 10 minutes | **Cook Time:** 15 minutes

Ingredients:

- 1 medium head cauliflower

- 2 tablespoons olive oil

- 1 small onion, finely chopped

- 2 cloves garlic, minced

- 1/2 cup carrots, finely diced

- 1/2 cup green peas (fresh or frozen)

- 1/4 cup chopped almonds or cashews

- 2 tablespoons raisins or dried cranberries

- 1 teaspoon ground cumin

- 1/2 teaspoon ground turmeric

- 1/2 teaspoon ground cinnamon

- Salt and black pepper, to taste

- 2 tablespoons fresh parsley or cilantro, chopped (for garnish)

Instructions:

1. Remove the leaves and stem from the cauliflower, and cut it into florets. Place the cauliflower florets in a food processor and pulse until they resemble rice or couscous-like grains. It would be advisable to do this in batches.

2. Heat olive oil in a large skillet or pan over medium heat. Add finely chopped onion and minced garlic, sautéing until softened and fragrant, about 2-3 minutes.

3. Add the cauliflower rice to the skillet, stirring to combine with the onion and garlic. Cook for about

5-6 minutes, stirring occasionally, until the cauliflower is tender but still slightly crisp.

4. Stir in finely diced carrots, green peas, chopped almonds or cashews, and raisins or dried cranberries. Cook for an additional 3-4 minutes, until the vegetables are heated through and the nuts are lightly toasted.

5. Season the cauliflower rice pilaf with ground cumin, ground turmeric, ground cinnamon, salt, and black pepper, stirring well to distribute the spices evenly.

6. Remove the skillet from heat and transfer the cauliflower rice pilaf to a serving dish.

7. Garnish with chopped fresh parsley or cilantro before serving.

8. Serve the Cauliflower Rice Pilaf hot as a flavorful and nutritious side dish or light meal.

Enjoy this wholesome and delicious Cauliflower Rice Pilaf, where the tender cauliflower grains are combined with a medley of vegetables, nuts, and aromatic spices, creating a satisfying and flavorful dish that's perfect for any occasion!

Cabbage and Pea Salad

Servings: 4 | **Prep Time:** 10 minutes | **Cook Time:** 0 minutes

Ingredients:

- 4 cups of green or red shredded cabbage

- 1 cup frozen peas, thawed

- 1/4 cup red onion, finely chopped

- 1/4 cup fresh parsley, chopped

- 2 tablespoons olive oil

- 2 tablespoons apple cider vinegar

- 1 tablespoon honey or maple syrup

- 1 teaspoon Dijon mustard

- Salt and black pepper, to taste

- Optional garnish: sesame seeds or chopped nuts

Instructions:

1. In a large mixing bowl, combine shredded cabbage, thawed peas, finely chopped red onion, and chopped fresh parsley.

2. In a small bowl, whisk together olive oil, apple cider vinegar, honey or maple syrup, Dijon mustard, salt, and black pepper to make the dressing.

3. Pour the dressing over the cabbage and pea mixture in the large mixing bowl. Toss gently to coat everything evenly.

4. Taste the salad and adjust seasoning if needed.

5. Transfer the Cabbage and Pea Salad to a serving dish.

6. Garnish with sesame seeds or chopped nuts if desired.

7. Serve immediately as a refreshing and nutritious side dish or light meal.

Enjoy the crisp and vibrant flavors of this Cabbage and Pea Salad, where the sweetness of peas complements the crunchy cabbage, creating a delightful harmony of taste and texture!

Kale Stuffed Peppers

Servings: 4 | **Prep Time:** 15 minutes | **Cook Time:** 30 minutes

Ingredients:

- 4 large bell peppers (any color), halved and seeds removed

- 1 tablespoon olive oil

- 1 small onion, diced

- 2 cloves garlic, minced

- 4 cups of chopped kale leaves with the stems removed

- 1 cup cooked quinoa

- 1 cup cooked black beans, drained and rinsed

- 1 teaspoon ground cumin

- 1/2 teaspoon smoked paprika

- Salt and black pepper, to taste

- 1 cup of shredded cheese it could be cheddar, mozzarella, or any of your preferred choice

- Optional garnish: chopped fresh parsley or cilantro

Instructions:

1. Preheat your oven to 375°F (190°C). Grease a baking dish large enough to hold the pepper halves.

2. Over medium heat, heat the olive oil in a large skillet. Add diced onion and minced garlic, sautéing until softened and fragrant, about 2-3 minutes.

3. Add chopped kale leaves to the skillet, stirring to combine with the onion and garlic. Cook for about 4-5 minutes until the kale is wilted and tender.

4. Stir in cooked quinoa, cooked black beans, ground cumin, smoked paprika, salt, and black pepper, mixing well to combine all the ingredients. Cook for an additional 2-3 minutes to heat through.

5. Arrange the bell pepper halves in the prepared baking dish, cut side up.

6. Spoon the kale, quinoa, and black bean mixture evenly into each bell pepper half, pressing it down gently.

7. Sprinkle shredded cheese over the top of each stuffed pepper.

8. Cover the baking dish with aluminum foil and bake in the preheated oven for 20-25 minutes, or

until the peppers are tender and the filling is heated through.

9. Remove the foil and bake for an additional 5 minutes to melt and lightly brown the cheese.

10. Remove from the oven and let the Kale Stuffed Peppers cool slightly before serving.

11. Garnish with chopped fresh parsley or cilantro if desired.

12. Serve hot as a satisfying and nutritious main dish.

Enjoy these delicious and wholesome Kale Stuffed Peppers, where tender bell peppers are filled with a flavorful mixture of kale, quinoa, black beans, and cheese, creating a hearty and satisfying meal that's perfect for any occasion!

Spicy Cabbage Soup

Servings: 6 | **Prep Time:** 15 minutes | **Cook Time:** 30 minutes

Ingredients:

- 1 tablespoon olive oil

- 1 onion, diced

- 2 cloves garlic, minced

- 1 teaspoon grated ginger

- 4 cups of green or red shredded cabbage

- 2 carrots, peeled and sliced

- 1 bell pepper, diced

- 1 can (14 oz) diced tomatoes

- 6 cups vegetable broth

- 1 teaspoon ground cumin

- 1/2 teaspoon chili powder

- 1/2 teaspoon paprika

- 1/4 teaspoon cayenne pepper (adjust to taste)

- Salt and black pepper, to taste

- Juice of 1 lime

- Chopped fresh cilantro or parsley, chopped, for extra garnish

- Sour cream or Greek yogurt (optional, for serving)

Instructions:

1. Dutch oven over medium heat. or heat olive oil in a large pot, for about 3-4 minutes, add diced onion and sauté until translucent.

2. Stir in minced garlic and grated ginger, and cook for another minute until fragrant.

3. Add shredded cabbage, sliced carrots, and diced bell pepper to the pot. Stirring occasionally, cook for about 5 minutes until you notice that the vegetables start to soften.

4. Pour in the diced tomatoes (with their juices) and vegetable broth. Add ground cumin, chili powder, paprika, cayenne pepper, salt, and black pepper. Stir to combine.

5. Bring the soup to a boil, then reduce the heat to low and let it simmer for 20-25 minutes, or until the vegetables are tender.

6. Stir in the lime juice and taste the soup. Adjust seasoning if needed, adding more salt, pepper, or cayenne pepper according to your preference.

7. Ladle the Spicy Cabbage Soup into bowls. Garnish with chopped fresh cilantro or parsley.

8. Serve hot, optionally topped with a dollop of sour cream or Greek yogurt for added creaminess.

CHAPTER FOUR– CUPCAKES RECIPES

Discover the magic of cupcakes with our delightful recipes! From classic flavors like vanilla and chocolate to creative twists with fruity or decadent toppings, these bite-sized treats are perfect for any occasion. Whether you're baking for a special celebration or simply craving a sweet indulgence, our recipes promise to satisfy your cravings and bring a smile to your face. So, grab your apron and let's bake up some happiness together!

Chocolate Avocado Cupcakes

Servings: 12 cupcakes | **Prep Time:** 15 minutes | **Bake Time:** 20 minutes

Ingredients:

- 1 ripe avocado, mashed (about 1/2 cup)

- 1/2 cup granulated sugar

- 1/4 cup unsweetened cocoa powder

- 1/4 cup of coconut milk

- 1 teaspoon vanilla extract

- 1 cup rice flour

- 1 teaspoon baking powder

- 1/2 teaspoon baking soda

- 1/4 teaspoon salt

- Chocolate chips or chopped nuts for garnish and its completely optional.

Instructions:

1. Preheat your oven to 350°F (175°C). With cupcake liners, line a 12-cup muffin tin.

2. In a mixing bowl, combine the mashed avocado and granulated sugar. Mix until smooth and well combined.

3. Add the unsweetened cocoa powder, milk, and vanilla extract to the bowl with the avocado mixture. Mix until smooth and creamy.

4. In a separate bowl, whisk together the rice flour, baking powder, baking soda, and salt.

5. Gradually add the dry ingredients to the wet ingredients, stirring until just combined. Be careful not to overmix.

6. Divide the batter evenly among the prepared cupcake liners, filling each about 3/4 full.

7. If desired, sprinkle chocolate chips or chopped nuts on top of each cupcake for added texture and flavor.

8. Bake in the preheated oven for 18-20 minutes, or until a toothpick inserted into the center of a cupcake comes out clean.

9. Remove the cupcakes from the oven and let them cool in the muffin tin for a few minutes before transferring them to a wire rack to cool completely.

10. Once cooled, frost the cupcakes with your favorite frosting or enjoy them as is.

11. Serve and enjoy these decadent Chocolate Avocado Cupcakes as a delightful treat!

Indulge in these moist and chocolatey cupcakes that are secretly infused with creamy avocado, adding richness and moisture to every bite. Perfect for chocolate lovers and health-conscious individuals alike, these cupcakes are sure to be a hit at any gathering!

Lemon Zest Cupcakes

Servings: 12 cupcakes | **Prep Time:** 15 minutes | **Bake Time:** 18-20 minutes

Ingredients:

- 1 1/2 cup rice flour

- 1 1/2 teaspoons baking powder

- 1/4 teaspoon salt

- 1/2 cup unsalted butter, softened

- 3/4 cup granulated sugar

- 1 teaspoon vanilla extract

- 1 tablespoon of lemon zest from about 2 lemons

- 1/4 cup fresh lemon juice

- 1/2 cup coconut milk

- Lemon slices, for garnish (optional)

For the Lemon Glaze:

- 1 cup powdered sugar

- 2-3 tablespoons fresh lemon juice

Instructions:

1. Preheat your oven to 350°F (175°C). With cupcake liners, line a 12-cup muffin tin.

2. Whisk together the rice flour, in a medium bowl, baking powder, and salt. Set aside.

3. In a large mixing bowl, beat the softened butter and granulated sugar together until light and fluffy.

4. Mix the vanilla extract and lemon zest until combined.

5. Gradually add the dry ingredients to the wet ingredients, alternating with the fresh lemon juice and milk, beginning and ending with the dry ingredients. Being careful not to overmix, you need to mix until just combined.

6. Divide the batter evenly among the prepared cupcake liners, filling each about 2/3 full.

7. Until a toothpick inserted into the center of a cupcake comes out clean, bake in the preheated oven for 18-20 minutes.

8. Remove the cupcakes from the oven and let them cool in the muffin tin for a few minutes before transferring them to a wire rack to cool completely.

9. While the cupcakes are cooling, prepare the lemon glaze. Whisk together the powdered sugar and fresh lemon juice until smooth, in a medium bowl.

10. Once the cupcakes are completely cooled, drizzle the lemon glaze over the top of each cupcake. For a few minutes, allow to glaze.

11. If desired, garnish each cupcake with a thin slice of lemon before serving.

12. Serve and enjoy these refreshing Lemon Zest Cupcakes as a delightful treat!

These Lemon Zest Cupcakes are bursting with bright citrus flavor and topped with a tangy lemon glaze, making them the perfect treat for any occasion. Light, fluffy, and full of zesty goodness, they're sure to brighten your day!

Red Velvet Beetroot Cupcakes

Servings: 12 cupcakes | **Prep Time:** 20 minutes | **Bake Time:** 18-20 minutes

Ingredients:

- 1 cup cooked and pureed beetroots (about 2 medium beetroots)

- 1/4 cup unsalted butter, melted

- 1/4 cup vegetable oil

- 3/4 cup granulated sugar

- 2 large eggs

- 1 teaspoon vanilla extract

- 1 1/4 cups rice flour

- 2 tablespoons unsweetened cocoa powder

- 1/2 teaspoon baking powder

- 1/4 teaspoon baking soda

- 1/4 teaspoon salt

- 1/4 cup buttermilk or plain yogurt or coconut milk

- 1 tablespoon red food coloring (optional)

- Cream cheese frosting, for topping

Instructions:

1. Preheat your oven to 350°F (175°C). With cupcake liners, line a 12-cup muffin tin with cupcake liners.

2. In a blender or food processor, puree the cooked beetroots until smooth. Measure out 1 cup of beetroot puree and set aside.

3. In a large mixing bowl, combine the melted butter, vegetable oil, and granulated sugar. Whisk until well combined.

4. Mixing well after each addition, add and stir in the vanilla extract.

5. In a separate bowl, sift together the rice flour, cocoa powder, baking powder, baking soda, and salt.

6. Mixing until just combined, gradually add all the dry ingredients to the wet ingredients.

7. Fold in the beetroot puree and buttermilk or plain yogurt until evenly incorporated. If desired, add red food coloring for a deeper red color.

8. Divide the batter evenly among the prepared cupcake liners, filling each about 2/3 full.

9. Bake in the preheated oven for 18-20 minutes, or until a toothpick inserted into the center of a cupcake comes out clean.

10. Remove the cupcakes from the oven and let them cool in the muffin tin for a few minutes before transferring them to a wire rack to cool completely.

11. Once the cupcakes are completely cooled, frost them with cream cheese frosting.

12. Serve and enjoy these delightful Red Velvet Beetroot Cupcakes!

Banana and Blueberry Cupcakes

Servings: 12 cupcakes | **Prep Time:** 15 minutes | **Bake Time:** 20-25 minutes

Ingredients:

- 1 1/2 cups rice flour

- 1 teaspoon baking powder

- 1/2 teaspoon baking soda

- 1/4 teaspoon salt

- 1/2 cup unsalted butter, softened

- 3/4 cup granulated sugar

- 1 teaspoon vanilla extract

- 2 ripe bananas, mashed

- 1/2 cup plain Greek yogurt or sour cream

- 1 cup fresh frozen, thawed and drained blueberries

- Optional: additional blueberries for topping

Instructions:

1. Preheat your oven to 350°F (175°C). With cupcake liners, line a 12-cup muffin tin with cupcake liners.

2. In a medium bowl, whisk together the rice flour, baking powder, baking soda, and salt. Set aside.

3. In a large mixing bowl, beat the softened butter and granulated sugar together until light and fluffy.

4. Mix in the vanilla extract.

5. Stir in the mashed bananas and plain Greek yogurt or sour cream until well combined.

6. Gradually add all of the dry ingredients to the wet ingredients, making sure that you mix well until just combined.

7. Gently fold in the fresh blueberries until evenly distributed throughout the batter.

8. Divide the batter evenly among the prepared cupcake liners, filling each about 2/3 full.

9. If desired, place a few additional blueberries on top of each cupcake for decoration.

10. Bake in the preheated oven for 20-25 minutes, or until a toothpick inserted into the center of a cupcake comes out clean.

11. Remove the cupcakes from the oven and let them cool in the muffin tin for a few minutes before transferring them to a wire rack to cool completely.

12. Once cooled, serve and enjoy these delicious Banana and Blueberry Cupcakes!

These Banana and Blueberry Cupcakes are moist, tender, and bursting with fruity flavor. The combination of ripe bananas and juicy blueberries creates a delightful treat that's perfect for any occasion. Enjoy them as a snack, dessert, or anytime treat!

Gingerbread Cupcakes

Servings: 12 cupcakes | **Prep Time:** 15 minutes | **Bake Time:** 18-20 minutes

Ingredients:

- 1 1/2 cups rice flour

- 1 teaspoon baking powder

- 1/2 teaspoon baking soda

- 1/4 teaspoon salt

- 1 teaspoon ground ginger

- 1 teaspoon ground cinnamon

- 1/4 teaspoon ground cloves

- 1/4 teaspoon ground nutmeg

- 1/2 cup unsalted butter, softened

- 1/2 cup brown sugar, packed

- 1/4 cup molasses

- 1/2 cup coconut milk

- 1 tablespoon apple cider vinegar

- 1 teaspoon vanilla extract

For the Cream Cheese Frosting:

- 8 oz cream cheese, softened

- 1/2 cup unsalted butter, softened

- 3-4 cups powdered sugar

- 1 teaspoon vanilla extract

Instructions:

1. Preheat your oven to 350°F (175°C). Next, with cupcake liners line a 12-cup muffin tin.

2. In a medium bowl, whisk together the rice flour, baking powder, baking soda, salt, ground ginger, ground cinnamon, ground cloves, and ground nutmeg. Set aside.

3. In a large mixing bowl, beat the softened butter and brown sugar together until light and fluffy.

4. Add the molasses, milk, apple cider vinegar, and vanilla extract to the bowl, mixing until combined.

5. Gradually add the of the dry ingredients into the wet ingredients, and mix until well combined.

6. Divide the batter evenly among the prepared cupcake liners, filling each about 2/3 full.

7. For about 18-20 minutes, bake in the preheated oven or until you put a toothpick into the center of the cupcake and it comes out clean.

8. Remove the cupcakes from the oven and let them cool in the muffin tin for a few minutes before transferring them to a wire rack to cool completely.

9. While the cupcakes are cooling, prepare the cream cheese frosting. In a large mixing bowl, you beat the already softened cream cheese and the unsalted butter together until it is very smooth and creamy.

10. Gradually add the powdered sugar, 1 cup at a time, mixing well after each addition, until the frosting reaches your desired consistency.

11. Stir in the vanilla extract until evenly incorporated.

12. Once the cupcakes are completely cooled, frost them with the cream cheese frosting.

13. Serve and enjoy these delightful Egg-Free Gingerbread Cupcakes!

These Egg-Free Gingerbread Cupcakes are perfect for those with egg allergies or dietary restrictions. With warm spices and rich molasses flavor, they're sure to be a hit at any festive gathering, whether you have food allergies or not!

Carrot and Apple Cupcake

Servings: 12 cupcakes | **Prep Time:** 15 minutes | **Bake Time:** 18-20 minutes

Ingredients:

- 1 1/2 cups rice flour

- 1 teaspoon baking powder

- 1/2 teaspoon baking soda

- 1/4 teaspoon salt

- 1 teaspoon ground cinnamon

- 1/4 teaspoon ground nutmeg

- 1/2 cup unsalted butter, softened

- 1/2 cup brown sugar, packed

- 1/4 cup honey or maple syrup

- 2 large grated carrots, it should be about one cup

- 1 medium apple, peeled and grated (about 1 cup)

- 1/2 cup unsweetened applesauce

- 1/4 cup coconut milk

- 1 teaspoon vanilla extract

For the Cream Cheese Frosting:

- 8 oz cream cheese, softened

- 1/4 cup unsalted butter, softened

- 2 cups powdered sugar

- 1 teaspoon vanilla extract

Instructions:

1. Preheat your oven to 350°F (175°C). using cupcake liners, line a 12-cup muffin tin.

2. In a medium bowl, whisk together the rice flour, baking powder, baking soda, salt, ground cinnamon, and ground nutmeg. Set aside.

3. In a large mixing bowl, beat the softened butter, brown sugar, and honey or maple syrup together until light and fluffy.

4. Add the grated carrots, grated apple, unsweetened applesauce, milk, and vanilla extract to the bowl, mixing until well combined.

5. Next, in a gradual manner add all the dry ingredients to the wet ingredients and mix until well combined.

6. Divide the batter evenly among the prepared cupcake liners, filling each about 2/3 full.

7. For about 18-20 minutes, bake in the preheated oven or until you insert a toothpick into the center of a cupcake and it comes out clean.

8. Remove the cupcakes from the oven and let them cool in the muffin tin for a few minutes before transferring them to a wire rack to cool completely.

9. While the cupcakes are cooling, prepare the cream cheese frosting. Using a large mixing bowl, beat your softened cream cheese as well as your unsalted butter together until they are smooth and creamy.

10. Gradually add the powdered sugar, 1/2 cup at a time, mixing well after each addition, until the frosting reaches your desired consistency.

11. Stir in the vanilla extract until evenly incorporated.

12. Once the cupcakes are completely cooled, frost them with the cream cheese frosting.

13. Serve and enjoy these delightful Carrot and Apple Cupcakes!

These Carrot and Apple Cupcakes are not only deliciously moist and flavorful but also meet the requirements of an EOE diet. With the natural sweetness of carrots and apples, they're a perfect treat for any occasion, whether you have food allergies or not!

CHAPTER FIVE– MUFFINS RECIPES

Muffins, those delightful handheld treats, are the epitome of simplicity and satisfaction. With their soft, tender crumb and endless flavor variations, muffins are a beloved staple of breakfast tables and coffee breaks worldwide. Whether enjoyed warm from the oven or packed for an on-the-go snack, muffins offer a comforting taste of home in every bite. From classic blueberry to decadent chocolate chip, muffins cater to every craving and occasion, making them a timeless favorite for all ages.

Apple Cinnamon Muffins

Servings: 12 muffins | **Prep Time:** 15 minutes | **Bake Time:** 18-20 minutes

Ingredients:

- 1 1/2 cups rice flour

- 1 teaspoon baking powder

- 1/2 teaspoon baking soda

- 1/4 teaspoon salt

- 1 teaspoon ground cinnamon

- 1/4 cup unsalted butter, melted

- 1/2 cup brown sugar, packed

- 1/4 cup honey or maple syrup

- 2 large apples, peeled and diced

- 1/2 cup unsweetened applesauce

- 1/4 cup of coconut milk

- 1 teaspoon vanilla extract

Instructions:

1. Preheat your oven to 350°F (175°C). Using paper liners, line a 12-cup muffin tin.

2. In a medium bowl, whisk together the rice flour, baking powder, baking soda, salt, and ground cinnamon. Set aside.

3. In a large mixing bowl, combine the melted butter, brown sugar, and honey or maple syrup. Mix until well combined.

4. Add the diced apples, unsweetened applesauce, milk, and vanilla extract to the bowl with the wet ingredients. Stir until evenly incorporated.

5. In a gradual manner, add all the dry ingredients to the wet ingredients, mixing until just combined. Be careful not to overmix.

6. Evenly divide the batter evenly among the already prepared muffin cups, filling each of them about 2/3 full.

7. Bake in the preheated oven for 18-20 minutes, or until a toothpick inserted into the center of a muffin comes out clean.

8. Remove the muffins from the oven and let them cool in the muffin tin for a few minutes before transferring them to a wire rack to cool completely.

9. Once cooled, serve and enjoy these delicious Apple Cinnamon Muffins!

These Apple Cinnamon Muffins are a delightful treat that's friendly for those following an EOE diet. Bursting with sweet apple chunks and warm cinnamon flavor, they're perfect for breakfast, snack time, or any moment you crave a comforting bite.

Berry Medley Muffins

Servings: 12 muffins | **Prep Time:** 15 minutes | **Bake Time:** 18-20 minutes

Ingredients:

- 1 1/2 cups rice flour

- 1 teaspoon baking powder

- 1/2 teaspoon baking soda

- 1/4 teaspoon salt

- 1/2 cup unsalted butter, melted

- 1/2 cup brown sugar, packed

- 1/4 cup honey or maple syrup

- 1/2 cup unsweetened applesauce

- 1/4 cup coconut milk

- 1 teaspoon vanilla extract

- 1 cup mixed berries (such as blueberries, raspberries, and diced strawberries), fresh or frozen

Instructions:

1. Preheat your oven to 350°F (175°C). Next, using paper liners, line a 12-cup muffin tin.

2. In a medium bowl, whisk together the rice flour, baking powder, baking soda, and salt. Set aside.

3. In a large mixing bowl, combine the melted butter, brown sugar, and honey or maple syrup. Mix until well combined.

4. Add the unsweetened applesauce, milk, and vanilla extract to the bowl with the wet ingredients. Stir until evenly incorporated.

5. Next, in a gradual manner, add all of the dry ingredients to the wet ingredients, and keep mixing until just combined. Be careful not to overmix.

6. Gently fold in the mixed berries until evenly distributed throughout the batter.

7. Divide the batter evenly among the prepared muffin cups, filling each about 2/3 full.

8. Bake in the preheated oven for 18-20 minutes, or until a toothpick inserted into the center of a muffin comes out clean.

9. Remove the muffins from the oven and let them cool in the muffin tin for a few minutes before transferring them to a wire rack to cool completely.

10. Once cooled, serve and enjoy these delightful Berry Medley Muffins!

These Berry Medley Muffins are a delicious treat that's friendly for those following an EOE diet. Bursting with a mix of juicy berries and sweetened with natural honey or maple syrup, they're perfect for breakfast, brunch, or any time you crave a wholesome snack.

Pear and Ginger Muffins

Servings: 12 muffins | **Prep Time:** 15 minutes | **Bake Time:** 18-20 minutes

Ingredients:

- 1 1/2 cups rice flour

- 1 teaspoon baking powder

- 1/2 teaspoon baking soda

- 1/4 teaspoon salt

- 1 teaspoon ground ginger

- 1/2 cup unsalted butter, melted

- 1/2 cup brown sugar, packed

- 1/4 cup honey or maple syrup

- 1/2 cup unsweetened applesauce

- 1/4 cup coconut milk

- 1 teaspoon vanilla extract

- 1 large peeled and diced ripe pear

Instructions:

1. Preheat your oven to 350°F (175°C). Using paper liners, line a 12-cup muffin tin.

2. In a medium bowl, whisk together the rice flour, baking powder, baking soda, salt, and ground ginger. Set aside.

3. In a large mixing bowl, combine the melted butter, brown sugar, and honey or maple syrup. Mix until well combined.

4. Add the unsweetened applesauce, milk, and vanilla extract to the bowl with the wet ingredients. Stir until evenly incorporated.

5. In a gradual manner, add all the dry ingredients to the wet ingredients, and make sure to properly mix until just combined. Be careful not to overmix.

6. Gently fold in the diced pear until evenly distributed throughout the batter.

7. Divide the batter evenly among the prepared muffin cups, filling each about 2/3 full.

8. Bake in the preheated oven for 18-20 minutes, or until a toothpick inserted into the center of a muffin comes out clean.

9. Remove the muffins from the oven and let them cool in the muffin tin for a few minutes before transferring them to a wire rack to cool completely.

10. Once cooled, serve and enjoy these delightful Pear and Ginger Muffins!

These Pear and Ginger Muffins are a delicious and EOE diet-friendly treat, combining the sweet, juicy flavor of pears with the warm, aromatic spice of ginger. Perfect for breakfast, brunch, or as a wholesome snack, these muffins are sure to become a favorite!

Raspberry and Coconut Muffins

Raspberry and Coconut Muffins Recipe (EOE Diet Friendly)

Servings: 12 muffins | Prep Time: 15 minutes | Bake Time: 18-20 minutes

Ingredients:

- 1 1/2 cups rice flour

- 1 teaspoon baking powder

- 1/2 teaspoon baking soda

- 1/4 teaspoon salt

- 1/2 cup unsalted butter, melted

- 1/2 cup brown sugar, packed

- 1/4 cup honey or maple syrup

- 1/2 cup unsweetened applesauce

- 1/4 cup coconut milk

- 1 teaspoon vanilla extract

- 1 cup fresh or frozen raspberries

- 1/2 cup shredded coconut, plus extra for topping

Instructions:

1. Preheat your oven to 350°F (175°C). Using s paper liner, line a 12-cup muffin tin.

2. In a medium bowl, whisk together the rice flour, baking powder, baking soda, and salt. Set aside.

3. In a large mixing bowl, combine the melted butter, brown sugar, and honey or maple syrup. Mix until well combined.

4. Add the unsweetened applesauce, milk, and vanilla extract to the bowl with the wet ingredients. Stir until evenly incorporated.

5. In a gradual manner mix, add all the dry ingredients to the wet ingredients, mix well until just combined. Be careful not to overmix.

6. Gently fold in the raspberries and shredded coconut until evenly distributed throughout the batter.

7. Divide the batter evenly among the prepared muffin cups, filling each about 2/3 full.

8. Sprinkle additional shredded coconut on top of each muffin, if desired.

9. For about 18-20 minutes, bake in the preheated oven, or until a you insert a toothpick into the center of a muffin and it comes out clean.

10. Remove the muffins from the oven and allow them to cool in the muffin tin for a few minutes before you transfer them to a wire rack to cool properly.

11. Once cooled, serve and enjoy these delightful Raspberry and Coconut Muffins!

These Raspberry and Coconut Muffins are a delicious and EOE diet-friendly treat, combining the tartness of raspberries with the sweet, tropical flavor of coconut. Perfect for breakfast, brunch, or as a wholesome snack, these muffins are sure to delight your taste buds!

Pear and Ginger Muffins

Servings: 12 muffins | **Prep Time:** 15 minutes | **Bake Time:** 18-20 minutes

Ingredients:

- 1 1/2 cups rice flour

- 1 teaspoon baking powder

- 1/2 teaspoon baking soda

- 1/4 teaspoon salt

- 1 teaspoon ground ginger

- 1/2 cup unsalted butter, melted

- 1/2 cup brown sugar, packed

- 1/4 cup honey or maple syrup

- 1/2 cup unsweetened applesauce

- 1/4 cup coconut milk

- 1 teaspoon vanilla extract

- 1 large peeled and diced ripe pear

Instructions:

1. Preheat your oven to 350°F (175°C). With paper liners, line a 12-cup muffin tin.

2. In a medium bowl, whisk together the rice flour, baking powder, baking soda, salt, and ground ginger. Set aside.

3. In a large mixing bowl, combine the melted butter, brown sugar, and honey or maple syrup. Mix until well combined.

4. Add the unsweetened applesauce, milk, and vanilla extract to the bowl with the wet ingredients. Stir until evenly incorporated.

5. Next, gradually add all of the dry ingredients to the wet ingredients, ensure to mix well until well combined. Be careful not to overmix.

6. Gently fold in the diced pear until evenly distributed throughout the batter.

7. Divide the batter evenly among the prepared muffin cups, filling each about 2/3 full.

8. Bake in the preheated oven for 18-20 minutes, or until a toothpick inserted into the center of a muffin comes out clean.

9. Remove the muffins from the oven and let them cool in the muffin tin for a few minutes before transferring them to a wire rack to cool completely.

10. Once cooled, serve and enjoy these delightful Pear and Ginger Muffins!

These Pear and Ginger Muffins are a delicious and EOE diet-friendly treat, combining the sweet, juicy flavor of pears with the warm, aromatic spice of ginger. Perfect for breakfast, brunch, or as a wholesome snack, these muffins are sure to become a favorite!

Pumpkin Muffins

Servings: 12 muffins | **Prep Time:** 15 minutes | **Bake Time:** 18-20 minutes

Ingredients:

- 1 1/2 cups rice flour

- 1 teaspoon baking powder

- 1/2 teaspoon baking soda

- 1/4 teaspoon salt

- 1 teaspoon ground cinnamon

- 1/2 teaspoon ground nutmeg

- 1/4 teaspoon ground cloves

- 1/2 cup unsalted butter, melted

- 1/2 cup brown sugar, packed

- 1/4 cup honey or maple syrup

- 1/2 cup unsweetened applesauce

- 1 cup of canned or even homemade pumpkin puree

- 1/4 cup milk (dairy or non-dairy)

- 1 teaspoon vanilla extract

Instructions:

1. Preheat your oven to 350°F (175°C). With paper liners, line a 12-cup muffin tin.

2. In a medium bowl, whisk together the rice flour, baking powder, baking soda, salt, ground cinnamon, ground nutmeg, and ground cloves. Set aside.

3. In a large mixing bowl, combine the melted butter, brown sugar, and honey or maple syrup. Mix until well combined.

4. Add the unsweetened applesauce, pumpkin puree, milk, and vanilla extract to the bowl with the wet ingredients. Stir until evenly incorporated.

5. Next, gradually add all of the dry ingredients to the wet ingredients, mixing well until just combined. Be careful not to overmix.

6. Evenly divide the batter among the prepared muffin cups, filling each of them about 2/3 full.

7. Bake in the preheated oven for 18-20 minutes, or until a toothpick inserted into the center of a muffin comes out clean.

8. Remove the muffins from the oven and let them cool in the muffin tin for a few minutes before transferring them to a wire rack to cool completely.

9. Once cooled, serve and enjoy these delightful Pumpkin Muffins!

These Pumpkin Muffins are a delicious and EOE diet-friendly treat, perfect for breakfast, brunch, or as a wholesome snack.

CONCLUSION

In closing, "**EOE Diet Cookbook:** Managing Food Allergies with Flavorful Recipes" is more than just a collection of recipes—it's a comprehensive guide designed to support individuals navigating Eosinophilic Esophagitis (EOE) and other food allergies. Through this cookbook, we've embarked on a journey to transform dietary restrictions into culinary opportunities, providing delicious and nutritious meal options that adhere to the 6FED (Six Food Elimination Diet) approach.

From the initial chapters offering an understanding of EOE and identifying dietary restrictions to stocking your EOE-friendly kitchen and mastering meal planning, this cookbook serves as a valuable resource for individuals and families alike. Each recipe is meticulously crafted with EOE dietary guidelines in mind, ensuring that everyone can enjoy flavorful meals without compromising their health or taste preferences.

Whether you're craving comforting classics like Pumpkin Muffins or exploring adventurous flavors with Raspberry and Coconut Muffins, every recipe in this cookbook celebrates the vibrant diversity of ingredients while prioritizing allergen-free options. With each bite, you'll discover a world of culinary delights that accommodate your dietary needs while tantalizing your taste buds.

As you embark on your journey with the "EOE Diet Cookbook," I extend my heartfelt gratitude to each reader and home cook. Your support and trust in this endeavor are truly appreciated. If this cookbook has enriched your culinary experience and eased the challenges of managing EOE and food allergies, I encourage you to share your thoughts by leaving an honest review. Your feedback not only helps us improve but also guides others in their journey towards a healthier and happier lifestyle.

Thank you for joining me on this culinary adventure. Together, let's continue to savor the joys of good food, good health, and good company. Happy cooking!

BONUS

In this part, there are 5 bonuses provided for you and they are;

BONUS ONE: 21 DAYS MEAL PLAN

Here's a 21-day meal plan for an EOE patient based on the recipes provided:

Day 1:

- **Breakfast:** Apple Cinnamon cauliflower rice Breakfast Bake

- **Lunch:** Avocado and Garbanzo Bean Quinoa Salad

- **Dinner:** Baked Chicken Taquitos with Strawberry Quinoa Salad with Feta

Day 2:

- **Breakfast:** Lemon Zest Cupcakes

- **Lunch:** Salsa Chicken Sheet Pan with Cabbage and Pineapple Stir-Fry

- Dinner: Italian Pork Sliders with Cherry Pecan Granola with Quinoa

Day 3:

- Breakfast: Banana and Blueberry Cupcakes

- Lunch: Asian Chicken Meatballs with Cauliflower Rice Pilaf

- Dinner: Slow Cooker Pork Tacos with Kale and Apple Salad

Day 4:

- Breakfast: Pumpkin Muffins

- Lunch: Creamy Lemon Chicken Pasta

- Dinner: San Francisco Pork Chops with Quinoa Porridge

Day 5:

- Breakfast: Chocolate Avocado Cupcakes

- Lunch: Broccoli Pesto Pasta with Broccoli and Avocado Salad

- Dinner: Beef and Quinoa Meatballs with Cabbage and Pea Salad

Day 6:

- Breakfast: Gingerbread Cupcakes

- Lunch: One Pan Mexican Mince and Rice with Kale Stuffed Peppers

- Dinner: Paprika Chicken Drumsticks with Spicy Cabbage Soup

Day 7:

- Breakfast: Berry Medley Muffins

- Lunch: Lemon Chicken Pasta with Kale Caesar Salad

- Dinner: Bacon Ramen Noodles with Apple Sausages Stuffed Butternut Squash

Day 8:

- Breakfast: Strawberry Quinoa Salad with Feta

- Lunch: Broccoli and Quinoa Casserole with Avocado and Garbanzo Bean Quinoa Salad

- **Dinner:** Baked Honey Mustard Chicken and Potatoes with Pear and Ginger Muffins

Day 9:

- **Breakfast:** Red Velvet Beetroot Cupcakes

- **Lunch:** Sausage and Peppers Pasta with Cabbage and Pineapple Stir-Fry

- **Dinner:** Lemon Zest Cupcakes with Raspberry and Coconut Muffins

Day 10:

- **Breakfast:** Quinoa Porridge

- **Lunch:** Kale and Apple Salad with San Francisco Pork Chops

- **Dinner:** Italian Pork Sliders with Cherry Pecan Granola with Quinoa

Day 11:

- **Breakfast:** Chocolate Avocado Cupcakes

- **Lunch:** Creamy Lemon Chicken Pasta with Broccoli and Avocado Salad

- Dinner: Beef and Quinoa Meatballs with Cabbage and Pea Salad

Day 12:

- Breakfast: Berry Medley Muffins

- Lunch: Salsa Chicken Sheet Pan with Cauliflower Rice Pilaf

- Dinner: Baked Chicken Taquitos with Strawberry Quinoa Salad with Feta

Day 13:

- Breakfast: Lemon Zest Cupcakes

- Lunch: Asian Chicken Meatballs with Kale Stuffed Peppers

- Dinner: Slow Cooker Pork Tacos with Quinoa Porridge

Day 14:

- Breakfast: Pumpkin Muffins

- Lunch: Broccoli Pesto Pasta with Avocado and Garbanzo Bean Quinoa Salad

- **Dinner:** Paprika Chicken Drumsticks with Spicy Cabbage Soup

Day 15:

- **Breakfast:** Banana and Blueberry Cupcakes

- **Lunch:** One Pan Mexican Mince and Rice with Kale Caesar Salad

- **Dinner:** Bacon Ramen Noodles with Apple Sausages Stuffed Butternut Squash

Day 16:

- **Breakfast:** Gingerbread Cupcakes

- **Lunch:** Italian Pork Sliders with Cherry Pecan Granola with Quinoa

- **Dinner:** Baked Honey Mustard Chicken and Potatoes with Pear and Ginger Muffins

Day 17:

- **Breakfast:** Strawberry Quinoa Salad with Feta

- **Lunch:** Creamy Lemon Chicken Pasta with Broccoli and Avocado Salad

- Dinner: Beef and Quinoa Meatballs with Cabbage and Pea Salad

Day 18:

- Breakfast: Chocolate Avocado Cupcakes

- Lunch: Sausage and Peppers Pasta with Cauliflower Rice Pilaf

- Dinner: Lemon Zest Cupcakes with Raspberry and Coconut Muffins

Day 19:

- Breakfast: Quinoa Porridge

- Lunch: Kale and Apple Salad with San Francisco Pork Chops

- Dinner: Baked Chicken Taquitos with Strawberry Quinoa Salad with Feta

Day 20:

- Breakfast: Red Velvet Beetroot Cupcakes

- Lunch: Broccoli Pesto Pasta with Avocado and Garbanzo Bean Quinoa Salad

- **Dinner:** Paprika Chicken Drumsticks with Spicy Cabbage Soup

Day 21:

- **Breakfast:** Berry Medley Muffins

- **Lunch:** Salsa Chicken Sheet Pan with Cauliflower Rice Pilaf

- **Dinner:** Slow Cooker Pork Tacos with Quinoa Porridge

Feel free to adjust the meal plan based on personal preferences and dietary needs. Enjoy your meals!

BONUS TWO: A Printable Meal Planner Template

This meal planner was specifically designed for managing EOE, along with shopping lists tailored to the recipes in the cookbook. This would help you to organize your meals and ingredients more efficiently while following the EOE Diet.

WEEKLY MEAL PLANNER

WEEK: | **DATE:**

MONDAY	TUESDAY	SHOPPING LIST

WEDNESDAY	THURSDAY

FRIDAY	SATURDAY

SUNDAY

WEEKLY MEAL PLANNER

WEEK:

DATE:

MONDAY	TUESDAY	SHOPPING LIST

WEDNESDAY	THURSDAY

FRIDAY	SATURDAY

SUNDAY

BONUS THREE: A COMPREHENSIVE GUIDE ...

This section deals with 'A COMPREHENSIVE GUIDE TO UNDERSTANDING FOOD LABELS AND IDENTIFYING POTENTIAL ALLERGENS OR HIDDEN SOURCES OF GLUTEN, DIARY, EGGS, FISH, SOY AND NUTS IN PACAKAGED FOODS'.

Understanding food labels and identifying potential allergens or hidden sources of common allergens like gluten, dairy, eggs, fish, soy, and nuts is crucial for individuals with food allergies, including those with Eosinophilic Esophagitis (EOE). Here's a comprehensive guide to help you navigate food labels effectively:

1. Start with the Ingredient List:

- The ingredient list provides a breakdown of all the components of the product.

- Look for common allergens such as wheat, milk, eggs, fish, soy, and nuts. These are often highlighted or mentioned in bold to draw attention.

- Be aware of less obvious names for allergens (e.g., whey for milk, albumin for eggs, and soy lecithin for soy).

- Watch out for cross-contamination warnings such as "may contain" or "processed in a facility that also processes" allergens.

2. Understand Allergen Labeling:

- In many countries, including the United States and Canada, regulations require manufacturers to clearly label major allergens in the ingredient list.

- Common allergens (e.g., milk, eggs, fish, shellfish, tree nuts, peanuts, wheat, and soybeans) must be explicitly stated either in the ingredient list or as a separate "Contains" statement.

- Pay close attention to any precautionary allergen statements, such as "may contain traces of," "processed in a facility that also processes," or "manufactured on shared equipment with."

3. Look for Gluten-Free Certification:

- For individuals with gluten sensitivity or celiac disease, look for products that are certified gluten-free.

- Gluten-free certification symbols (e.g., the GF logo or a statement like "certified gluten-free") indicate that the product has undergone testing and meets specific gluten-free standards.

4. Beware of Hidden Sources:

- Some ingredients may contain hidden sources of allergens:

- Milk derivatives like casein or whey can be found in processed foods, flavorings, and baked goods.

- Egg products may appear in baked goods, pasta, and certain sauces.

- Fish sauce, Worcestershire sauce, and certain condiments may contain fish.

- Soy can hide in a variety of products under names like soybean oil, soy lecithin, and soy protein.

- Nuts can be present in many forms, including oils, flours, and extracts.

5. Utilize Allergen Apps and Resources:

- There are several mobile apps and online resources available to help identify allergens in packaged foods. These tools can scan barcodes and provide detailed allergen information.

6. Consult with Food Allergy Specialists:

- If you have specific concerns about allergens or dietary restrictions, consult with a registered dietitian specializing in food allergies or a food allergy specialist.

7. Stay Informed and Advocate for Yourself:

- Keep up-to-date with food labeling regulations and be proactive in advocating for your dietary needs.

- When in doubt, contact the manufacturer directly for clarification on ingredients and potential allergen cross-contamination.

By understanding food labels and being diligent in identifying potential allergens or hidden sources of common allergens, individuals with food allergies, including those with EOE, can make informed choices and maintain a safe and enjoyable diet.

BONUS FOUR: A PERSONALIZED RECIPE CONSULTATION

My email will be provided below to enable you send me messages so as to have a personal recipe consultation via email.

Readers could submit their dietary restrictions and preferences, and the cookbook author which is me would provide tailored recipe recommendations and suggestions to help you create delicious and safe meals that suit your individual needs. This personalized service would give you the opportunity to receive customized guidance and support in navigating your EoE diet, empowering you to feel confident and inspired in the kitchen. You can contact me via this email-

sophiacampbell.nutrition@gmail.com

BONUS FIVE: INGREDIENT SUBSTITUTION GUIDE

Here's an extended and detailed ingredient substitution guide tailored specifically for individuals with Eosinophilic Esophagitis (EOE) following an EOE diet: Living with Eosinophilic Esophagitis (EOE) often requires strict adherence to an EOE diet, which involves eliminating specific allergens and potential triggers from your meals. Here's a comprehensive guide to ingredient substitutions that will help you navigate your EOE diet with confidence and creativity.

1. Milk/Dairy Substitutions:

- Many individuals with EOE are advised to avoid dairy products due to lactose intolerance or dairy allergies. Luckily, there are a lot of dairy-free alternatives available.

- **Substitutions:** Opt out for unsweetened almond milk, coconut milk, soy milk, oat milk, rice milk, or hemp milk as replacements for cow's milk.

- **Tips:** Choose fortified varieties to ensure you're still getting essential nutrients like calcium and vitamin D. Unsweetened versions are preferable to minimize added sugars.

2. Egg Substitutions:

- Eggs are a common allergen and may need to be eliminated from your EOE diet. Luckily, there are several egg alternatives that work well in baking and cooking.

- **Substitutions:** Try using unsweetened applesauce, mashed banana, or a flaxseed meal or chia seed mixture (1 tablespoon of seeds mixed with 3 tablespoons of water, allowed to sit until gel-like) as egg replacements.

- **Tips:** Experiment with different substitutes to find the best option for each recipe. Keep in mind that some substitutions may alter the texture or flavor slightly.

3. Wheat/Gluten Substitutions:

- Wheat and gluten-containing grains are often problematic for individuals with EOE. Luckily, there are a lot of gluten-free alternatives that are available.

- **Substitutions:** Replace wheat flour with gluten-free alternatives such as rice flour, almond flour, coconut flour, tapioca flour, or a gluten-free all-purpose flour blend.

- **Tips:** Gluten-free baking may require additional binders like xanthan gum or guar gum to achieve the desired texture. Follow recipes specifically developed for gluten-free baking for best results.

4. Fish Substitutions:

- Fish allergies are common among individuals with EOE, necessitating the need for fish-free alternatives in recipes.

- **Substitutions:** Swap fish with seafood alternatives such as shrimp, scallops, lobster, or even plant-based options like tofu, tempeh, or jackfruit.

- **Tips:** Be cautious of fish-derived ingredients like fish sauce or fish stock in sauces and condiments. Look for vegan or plant-based alternatives when needed.

5. Soy Substitutions:

- Soy allergies can pose challenges for individuals following an EOE diet, but there are plenty of soy-free alternatives available.

- **Substitutions:** Replace soy sauce with tamari (gluten-free soy sauce), coconut amino, or liquid amino. Tofu can be substituted with chickpeas, beans, seitan, or other plant-based proteins.

- Tips: Check ingredient labels carefully for hidden sources of soy, such as soy lecithin or soy protein isolate, especially in processed foods.

6. Nut Substitutions:

- Nut allergies are prevalent and may require strict avoidance of nuts and nut-derived products.

- Substitutions: Sunflower seeds, pumpkin seeds, sesame seeds, hemp seeds, or toasted coconut flakes can often be used as nut replacements in recipes.

- Tips: Be vigilant about cross-contamination in manufacturing facilities when selecting alternative products. Look for nut-free certifications when necessary.

7. Shellfish Substitutions:

- Shellfish allergies can be severe and require careful avoidance of shellfish-containing foods.

- Substitutions: Swap shellfish with alternative seafood options like fish, shrimp, scallops, or even plant-based alternatives like tofu, tempeh, or jackfruit.

- Tips: Avoid seafood broths, stocks, or sauces that may contain shellfish derivatives. Read ingredient labels meticulously for hidden sources of shellfish.

8. Additional Tips for Ingredient Substitutions:

- Experimentation is key: Don't be afraid to try new ingredients and combinations to find what works best for your palate and dietary needs.

- Use caution with processed foods: Always read labels carefully, as allergens and hidden ingredients may be present in packaged foods.

- Reach out to healthcare professionals: Consult with a registered dietitian or allergist for personalized advice and recommendations tailored to your specific dietary restrictions and health goals.

By utilizing this comprehensive ingredient substitution guide, you can confidently navigate your EOE diet while still enjoying a wide variety of delicious and nutritious meals. Remember to listen to your body and make adjustments as needed to ensure optimal health and well-being on your EOE journey.

MEASUREMENTS AND CONCLUSION TABLE

1. Volume Measurements:

- 1 teaspoon (tsp) = 5 milliliters (ml)

- 1 tablespoon (tbsp) = 15 milliliters (ml)

- 1 fluid ounce (fl oz) = 29.57 milliliters (ml)

- 1 cup = 240 milliliters (ml)

- 1 pint (16 fl oz) = 473 milliliters (ml)

- 1 quart (32 fl oz) = 946 milliliters (ml)

- 1 gallon (128 fl oz) = 3.785 liters (L)

2. Weight Measurements:

- 1 ounce (oz) = 28.35 grams (g)

- 1 pound (lb) = 16 ounces = 453.59 grams (g)

- 1 kilogram (kg) = 2.205 pounds (lbs)

3. Dry Ingredients:

- 1 cup all-purpose flour = 120 grams (g)

- 1 cup granulated sugar = 200 grams (g)

- 1 cup brown sugar = 220 grams (g)

- 1 cup powdered sugar = 125 grams (g)

- 1 cup rolled oats = 90 grams (g)

- 1 cup nuts (chopped) = 115 grams (g)

- 1 cup breadcrumbs = 100 grams (g)

4. Liquid Ingredients:

- 1 cup water = 240 milliliters (ml)

- 1 cup milk = 240 milliliters (ml)

- 1 cup buttermilk = 240 milliliters (ml)

- 1 cup vegetable oil = 240 milliliters (ml)

5. Temperature Conversions:

- 350°F = 175°C (moderate oven)

- 375°F = 190°C (moderately hot oven)

- 400°F = 200°C (hot oven)

- 425°F = 220°C (very hot oven)

6. Miscellaneous Conversions:

- **1 stick of butter** = 1/2 cup = 113 grams (g)

- **1 clove of garlic** = approximately 1/2 teaspoon minced

- **1 medium-sized onion** = approximately 1 cup chopped

- **1 lemon** = approximately 2-3 tablespoons of juice

Made in United States
Troutdale, OR
02/16/2025